PRICE ACTION INSIGHTS

"HARNESSING THE POWER OF PRICE ACTION TRADING" - FROM VISION TO VICTORY

HAFFIZULLA KHAN

Made with ♥ on the Notion Press Platform
www.notionpress.com

To my beloved family, who have stood by me at every turn, offering unwavering support and love throughout this journey. To my mentors, whose guidance has been invaluable, and to my students, from whom I have learned just as much as I hope to teach. To my friends, both near and far, who have inspired me with their belief in my vision, despite the distance between us. This book is a testament to your encouragement and faith, which have fueled my passion for trading and writing. Thank you all for being my life's pillars of strength and motivation.

To those who have walked this journey alongside me, each of you has left an indelible mark on my heart and my life.

To my loved ones, who have believed in me through every step, every high, and every low. Your unwavering faith has been my foundation, a constant source of strength, and a reminder that no success is truly mine alone. Your love has sustained me, giving me the courage to push forward even in the darkest hours.

To my mentors, those wise guides who have given me not only knowledge but the insight, patience, and resilience that true mastery demands. You have taught me to view trading not only as a skill but as a craft, something to refine continuously with discipline and dedication. I am forever grateful for your generous guidance, which has shaped me into the person and professional I am today.

To my students, each of whom has allowed me the privilege of teaching. Through teaching, I have learned humility, patience, and the profound responsibility that comes with imparting knowledge. You have pushed me to better understand, to dive deeper, and to explain concepts in ways that bring them to life. Your growth has been my reward, and your trust in me has inspired me to keep striving.

To my family, whose unconditional support has been my safety net and my motivation. You stood by me through every struggle, celebrated every victory, and offered a shoulder whenever I stumbled. This book, this journey, would have been impossible without the strength and love you have given me. You are the heart of everything I do, and my success is as much yours as it is mine.

To my friends, both near and far. Though distance has sometimes separated us, your support and encouragement have been constant. You have been the voice cheering me on, reminding me of the value of true friendship and how it can transcend miles. Your belief in me has been invaluable, and I am forever thankful.

To everyone—friends, colleagues, and supporters—who have played a role in this journey, no matter how big or small. This book stands as a testament to all that you have given me, and it is my humble hope that it reflects the values and lessons you have taught me. May it serve as a small repayment for the profound impact each of you has had on my life.

With love, respect, and heartfelt gratitude, thank you all. You are, and always will be, the heart of my journey.

Contents

FOREWORD

I, Haffizulla Khan, was born and raised in the vibrant city of Bangalore, where my journey into the world of trading began. It was a path filled with curiosity, determination, and the unwavering belief that understanding the markets could lead to a life of fulfillment and success. Over the past six years, I have had the honor of mentoring over 3,000 students and clients across various markets—Indian, forex, and cryptocurrency. Each interaction, each story, has enriched my life and fueled my passion for sharing knowledge.

This book, Price Action Insights, is not merely a collection of trading techniques; it is a heartfelt message to every aspiring trader who has ever felt lost or overwhelmed in this complex world. It pains me deeply to witness the struggles of those who venture into trading, often losing their hard-earned money due to a lack of proper education and guidance. This heartache has driven me to put pen to paper, to share the insights I've gathered and to extend a hand to those who seek a better understanding of the markets.

Trading can often feel like a solitary journey, filled with moments of doubt and frustration. It is easy to be swayed by the allure of quick profits, yet I want to emphasize that real success in trading comes from patience, persistence, and a willingness to learn. Too many people fall into the trap of seeking instant gratification, neglecting the importance of education and experience. This book serves as a reminder that true mastery takes time and dedication, and it is my hope that readers will find comfort in knowing they are not alone on this path.

Price action—the foundation of my trading philosophy—holds the key to understanding the market's true nature. The price reflects the collective emotions, decisions, and behaviors of all participants. It tells a story that, when understood, empowers traders to make informed decisions. I encourage you to immerse yourself in this narrative, to learn to read the charts as you would a book, unraveling the emotions and motivations behind each movement.

Through these pages, I aim to instill a sense of hope and resilience in every reader. I want you to know that every setback is an opportunity for growth and that each loss is a lesson in disguise. The market has a way of humbling us, teaching us the value of discipline and the importance of risk management. It demands respect, patience, and an unwavering commitment to continuous improvement.

As you embark on this journey with me, remember that trading is not just about financial gain; it is about personal growth, self-discovery, and the relentless pursuit of knowledge. The insights shared in this book are meant to guide you, to inspire you, and to remind you that the path to success is paved with hard work, perseverance, and an open heart.

Thank you for allowing me to be part of your journey. Together, let us embrace the challenges, celebrate the victories, and cultivate a community of traders who uplift and support one another. May this book serve as a beacon of knowledge and encouragement as you navigate the fascinating world of trading.

PREFACE

Trading is an art and a science, a delicate balance that requires not only technical skill but also a deep understanding of human psychology. It demands dedication, patience, and an unwavering willingness to learn. My journey in this field began over six years ago in the vibrant city of Bangalore, where I first discovered my passion for price action trading. It was a path that would lead me through both triumphs and tribulations, shaping not only my skills as a trader but also my perspective on life and resilience.

Since that initial spark, I have had the privilege of training more than 3,000 students and clients across various markets, including Indian stocks, forex, and cryptocurrencies. Each interaction has been a unique opportunity to share knowledge and foster growth, but it has also been a reminder of the challenges many traders face. Throughout my experience, I have witnessed countless individuals entering the market with high hopes, only to find themselves overwhelmed by the harsh realities of trading.

It truly breaks my heart to see hard-earned money go to waste due to a lack of proper education and understanding. The pain of losing financial stability can be devastating, not just for the individual but also for their families. This realization has driven me to share my knowledge and insights through this book. My hope is to reach aspiring traders and illuminate the path to success, helping them recognize that true achievement in trading does not stem from chasing quick profits. Instead, it comes from a profound understanding of the market, honing one's skills, and implementing effective risk management strategies.

In Price Action Insights, I aim to equip you with the essential tools and knowledge needed to read price action and make informed decisions. You will learn to interpret charts with confidence, understand market behavior, and develop a personalized trading strategy that resonates with your unique style. This book is designed to empower you with the skills to navigate the often turbulent waters of the financial markets, steering clear of the pitfalls that ensnare so many traders.

Trading is not just about numbers; it is about interpreting a narrative that unfolds on the charts. Each price movement tells a story of buyers and sellers, hopes and fears, and market dynamics at play. By learning to read this narrative, you gain insight into the underlying forces that drive market movements. My goal is to demystify this process, providing clarity and direction as you embark on your trading journey.

As you delve into the chapters ahead, I encourage you to embrace the learning process with an open mind. Be patient with yourself, as every successful trader was once a beginner navigating the complexities of the market. Understand that setbacks are not failures; they are valuable lessons that contribute to your growth. Trading requires a mindset that is adaptable and resilient, one that sees challenges as stepping stones rather than obstacles.

I invite you to embark on this journey with me. Together, let us cultivate a community of traders who uplift and support one another. The world of trading can often feel isolating, but it doesn't have to be. As you explore the insights within this book, I hope you find encouragement and motivation to keep pushing forward, even in the face of adversity.

Thank you for choosing to read Price Action Insights. May it serve as a valuable resource in your trading journey, illuminating the path to success and empowering you to become a confident and skilled trader.

Acknowledgements

As I reflect on the journey that has led to the creation of Price Action Insights, I am overwhelmed with gratitude for the many individuals who have contributed to this endeavor in profound ways.

First and foremost, I want to express my deepest appreciation to my family. Your unwavering support and encouragement have been my anchor throughout my journey as a trader and educator. You have celebrated my victories and comforted me in my struggles, reminding me that I am never alone. Your belief in my dreams has fueled my motivation and inspired me to reach heights I once thought unattainable. Thank you for being my steadfast pillars of strength.

To my mentors, I extend my heartfelt gratitude for your invaluable guidance. Your wisdom, patience, and insights have been instrumental in shaping my understanding of trading. You have opened my eyes to the possibilities within this field and ignited a passion within me to share that knowledge with others. Your belief in me has encouraged me to push the boundaries of my potential, and for that, I am eternally grateful.

To my students and clients, thank you for placing your trust in me. Your dedication and eagerness to learn have motivated me to write this book. The privilege of training and learning alongside you has been one of the greatest joys of my career. Each of you has taught me something unique, and your growth as traders inspires me daily. I hope this book serves as a testament to your hard work and a guide on your journey to success.

I cannot forget my long-distance friends, who have been my emotional support system. Your love, encouragement, and reminders of our shared goals have brought warmth to my heart during challenging times. Even miles apart, you have reminded me that true friendship knows no distance. Thank you for believing in me and for being there when I needed it most.

Lastly, I wish to acknowledge everyone who has contributed indirectly to this book. Your encouragement and support, whether through kind words or thoughtful gestures, have made a significant impact on my work and my life. Each of you has played a part in this journey, and I am deeply grateful.

This book is dedicated to all of you. Your belief in me has made this journey possible, and I hope it serves as a reflection of the love and support that has surrounded me. May we all continue to inspire and uplift each other as we navigate our individual paths.

PROLOGUE

In the fast-paced world of trading, where the stakes are high and emotions run deep, many aspiring traders often find themselves lost in a maze of complex strategies and technical jargon. It can be overwhelming, and I know this feeling all too well. Like many of you, I have walked this path and faced my share of challenges, setbacks, and moments of doubt. I have experienced the highs of victory and the lows of failure, and it is through this journey that I discovered the transformative power of understanding price action—the real heartbeat of the market.

This book, Price Action Insights, is a culmination of my experiences as a trader and educator over the past six years. It represents not only my journey but also the journeys of thousands of students and clients across the globe whom I have had the privilege of working with. Each one has come to me with their own dreams, struggles, and aspirations in the intricate world of trading. My mission has always been clear: to empower traders with the knowledge and skills necessary to succeed while helping them avoid the common pitfalls that can lead to financial loss.

Reflecting on my journey, I am deeply moved by the stories of traders who have sought my guidance. Many enter the market with dreams of quick riches, fueled by the allure of financial freedom. They are often met with harsh realities that shatter those dreams. The emotional turmoil of experiencing losses, frustration, and self-doubt can be devastating. It is this emotional struggle that compelled me to write this book. I want to share not only my insights but also the lessons I have learned through years of practice and observation.

Price Action Insights is designed to be a practical guide for traders at all levels, from beginners who are just starting to explore the markets to seasoned professionals looking to refine their strategies. Here, you will find straightforward explanations of key concepts, actionable strategies, and real-world examples that illustrate the power of price action. I believe that understanding how to read the market is crucial for developing the confidence needed to make informed trading decisions and ultimately achieve financial goals.

Throughout this book, I will draw upon the experiences of successful traders—individuals who have navigated the turbulent waters of the financial markets and emerged victorious. Their stories will serve as both inspiration and cautionary tales, reminding us that the road to success is often paved with challenges. By learning from their experiences, you can avoid common mistakes and cultivate the mindset necessary for long-term success.

Join me on this journey as we delve into the world of price-action trading. Together, we will uncover the patterns, behaviors, and strategies that can lead to success in the markets. I invite you to approach this book with an open mind and a willingness to learn. Trading is not just a skill; it is an art that requires dedication, patience, and a continuous desire to improve. Embrace the learning process, stay committed to your growth, and remember: every successful trader was once a beginner.

Thank you for choosing to embark on this journey with me. May this book serve as a valuable resource that not only guides you in your trading endeavors but also inspires you to achieve your dreams.

I

Introduction to Trading and Markets

Trading has become a popular way for people to grow their wealth and reach financial goals, but it can initially seem complex. This chapter is designed to help you understand what trading is, how financial markets work, and why price action is a powerful approach to trading.

What is Trading?

Trading involves buying and selling financial assets—such as stocks, foreign currencies (forex), or cryptocurrencies—to make a profit. Think of it as buying a product when the price is low and then selling it when it goes up. In trading, these "products" are financial assets, whose prices move up and down based on various factors, including economic news, company earnings, and even global events.

In general, people trade for two main reasons:

1. Investing for Long-Term Growth: Some traders buy assets and hold onto them for months or years, hoping they will grow in value over time.

2. Making Short-Term Profits: Others aim to profit from price changes within shorter periods, such as hours, days, or weeks.

Types of Financial Markets

There are several types of markets where trading happens. Each one has unique features, but they all share a common goal: connecting buyers and sellers.

1. Stock Market: The stock market is where people buy and sell shares of publicly traded companies, such as Apple, Tesla, or Google. When you buy a share of a company, you are buying a small ownership in it. If the company grows, your share could become more valuable.

2. Forex Market: The forex (foreign exchange) market is where people trade currencies. This is the largest financial market in the world, with daily trading volumes exceeding $6 trillion. Traders in the forex market buy one currency while selling another, hoping to profit from changes in exchange rates.

3. Cryptocurrency Market: The cryptocurrency market is relatively new and allows people to trade digital currencies like Bitcoin and Ethereum. Cryptocurrencies are decentralized, meaning they are not controlled by a central authority like a government or bank.

Each of these markets has its own characteristics, but they all involve buying assets at one price and selling at another to make a profit.

Basic Terms in Trading

Before going further, let's cover some key terms in trading. Understanding these terms will help you follow along as we dive deeper into trading strategies and techniques.

1. Bullish: This term means that a trader expects prices to go up. For example, if someone says "I am bullish on Apple," it means they think Apple's share price will increase.

2. Bearish: This is the opposite of bullish. A bearish trader expects prices to go down. Saying "I am bearish on Bitcoin" means the trader thinks the price of Bitcoin will fall.

3. Volatility: Volatility refers to how much an asset's price moves over time. High volatility means the price changes a lot in a short period, which can offer more chances to make profits but also comes with more risk. Low volatility means the price moves slowly and predictably.

4. Liquidity: Liquidity is how easily an asset can be bought or sold. Assets with high liquidity, like major stocks or popular currencies, are easy to trade quickly without affecting their prices. Assets with low liquidity can be harder to sell quickly and may require the seller to accept a lower price.

5. Ask Price: The price that sellers are willing to accept for an asset. This is the price at which you can buy the asset from a seller.

6. Bid Price: The price that buyers are willing to pay for an asset. This is the price at which you can sell the asset to a buyer.

7. Spread: The difference between the bid price and the ask price. A smaller spread usually means the asset has high liquidity, while a larger spread can indicate lower liquidity.

8. Leverage: Leverage allows traders to control a larger position with a smaller amount of money. For example, a 1:10 leverage means that for every $1 in your account, you can control $10 in the market. While it increases potential gains, it also increases potential losses.

9. Margin: The amount of money needed in your trading account to open a leveraged position. Margin acts as a "deposit" to cover any potential losses.

10. Pip (Percentage in Point): A pip is the smallest price movement in currency trading. For most forex pairs, it's the fourth decimal place. For example, if EUR/USD moves from 1.1050 to 1.1051, it has moved one pip.

11. Stop Loss: An order to automatically sell an asset when it reaches a certain price. This helps limit potential losses by closing a trade before the price falls further.

12. Take Profit: An order to automatically sell an asset when it reaches a certain profit level. This locks in gains by closing the trade when it hits a pre-set price.

Order Types

1. Market Order: A buy or sell order to be executed immediately at the current market price.

2. Limit Order: An order to buy or sell at a specific price. A buy-limit order is placed below the current market price, while a sell-limit order is placed above the current price.

3. Liquidity Provider: Financial institutions or individuals that provide liquidity (buy and sell orders) in the market. High liquidity often leads to smaller spreads and more stable prices.

4. Slippage: This occurs when an order is executed at a different price than expected. Slippage can happen during times of high volatility or low liquidity.

5. Swing Trading: A trading style that involves holding positions for several days or weeks to capture medium-term price movements.

6. Day Trading: A trading style where positions are opened and closed within the same day, avoiding overnight exposure.

7. Scalping: A very short-term trading style that involves making quick trades, often lasting just seconds or minutes, to capture small price changes.

8. Position Size: The number of units of an asset you hold in a trade. Position sizing is an important part of risk management as it determines how much money is at risk in each trade.

9. Bull Market vs. Bear Market:

Bull Market: A market where prices are rising or expected to rise.

Bear Market: A market where prices are falling or expected to fall.

10. Breakout: When the price of an asset moves above a resistance level or below a support level, often signaling a new trend direction.

11. Risk-to-Reward Ratio: A ratio that compares the potential profit of a trade to its potential loss. For example, a risk-to-reward ratio of 1:3 means you are willing to risk $1 to potentially earn $3.

Introduction to Price Action Trading

Price action trading is a way of analyzing and trading the markets by looking at the asset's price movement over time, without relying heavily on indicators or complex tools. It's a straightforward approach, where traders focus on reading and understanding price changes through charts.

In price action trading, traders analyze:

Candlestick Patterns: These show price changes over time and help traders understand market sentiment.

Support and Resistance Levels: These are prices at which an asset tends to stop and reverse its direction.

Trends: Trends show the general direction of the price over a certain period.

By observing these elements, traders make predictions about where the price might go next. Price action traders believe that everything you need to know is reflected in the price itself, so instead of looking at lots of technical indicators, they focus directly on price movements.

Why Price Action Matters

One reason price action is so popular is that it is universal—it can be applied to any market, whether stocks, forex, or cryptocurrencies. Because it's based on price movement alone, it doesn't require complex calculations or advanced indicators. It's a skill that anyone can learn with practice, and it gives traders a way to react to the market in real-time rather than relying on delayed signals.

Price action also helps traders avoid what is called "analysis paralysis," where too many indicators can create confusion and hesitation. By focusing only on price, traders can make decisions faster and with more confidence.

Key Takeaways for New Traders

As you start your trading journey, remember that trading is not a "get rich quick" scheme. It requires learning, patience, and practice. Here are a few important points to keep in mind:

1. Educate Yourself: Take the time to learn the basics and understand how each market works. Knowledge is your best tool in trading.

2. Practice on a Demo Account: Many trading platforms offer demo accounts where you can practice trading with virtual money. This helps you gain experience without risking real money.

3. Start Small: Once you feel ready to trade with real money, start with a small amount. This allows you to learn from any mistakes without a significant financial loss.

4. Use Risk Management: Successful traders know how to manage risk. This means not betting all your money on one trade and setting "stop-loss" orders to minimize potential losses.

5. Avoid Greed: Greed is one of the quickest ways to lose money in trading. When you're overly focused on making huge profits, you might take unnecessary risks. Stick to your plan and target realistic, achievable goals

rather than chasing big wins every time.

6. Be Patient: Trading success takes time and experience. Don't expect overnight success, and remember that consistency in small gains can be more rewarding in the long run than attempting high-risk moves for quick profits.

7. Trust Your Mentors: Learning from those with more experience is invaluable. Mentors can offer insights from years of experience and help you avoid costly mistakes. Even if you feel confident, their guidance can be a powerful resource, especially when the market gets unpredictable.

8. Backtest Your Strategies: Before trading with real money, test your strategies on historical data to see how they would have performed in the past. Backtesting helps you refine your approach and gain confidence in your strategies. The more data you use, the better you'll understand how your strategy works in different market conditions.

9. Continuous Practice: The market is constantly evolving, so practice should be continuous. Use demo accounts to test new strategies and adapt to changing trends without risking real capital. The more you practice, the better prepared you'll be for the live market.

10. Focus on Risk Management: Trading isn't just about profits; it's about managing losses. Use tools like stop-loss orders and only risk a small portion of your capital on each trade. Proper risk management helps protect your account from significant losses, allowing you to stay in the game longer.

OUR CONTACT LINKS

[**WWW.RETROTRADING.ONLINE**] OUR WEBSITE

RETRO_TRADING_ [INSTA]

[https://www.instagram.com/retro_trading_/profilecard/?igsh=N3hvaWNlbGo4bGd2]

II

Understanding Price Action

In trading, "price action" refers to the movement of an asset's price on a chart. It's often analyzed without indicators, focusing purely on historical prices to anticipate future movements. Understanding price action is foundational for many professional traders, as it reveals the collective psychology of buyers and sellers. This chapter will break down the key concepts behind price action and explain how top traders analyze it.

1. What is Price Action?

Price action is the analysis of price movements over time. Unlike using indicators (like RSI or MACD), price action focuses solely on the current and historical price levels, often by observing candlestick patterns and support/resistance levels. Traders believe that everything affecting the price — news, economic indicators, and trader sentiment — is already reflected in price movements.

2. Why Focus on Price Action?

Many top traders believe that price action provides a purer form of market analysis. Instead of relying on lagging indicators, they look at real-time data to gauge momentum and trend strength. By understanding price action, traders can make quicker decisions and respond to market shifts without waiting for indicators to confirm a move.

3. Core Concepts of Price Action

A. Trends

Price action relies heavily on identifying trends. There are three main types:

Uptrend: A series of higher highs and higher lows, indicating buyers' dominance.

Downtrend: A series of lower lows and lower highs, suggesting sellers are in control.

Sideways Trend (Range): Prices move horizontally between support and resistance levels, showing a balance between buyers and sellers.

B. Support and Resistance

Support is a price level where buying interest tends to prevent further declines.

Resistance is a level where selling interest limits price increases. These levels often represent psychological price points where traders expect significant movement.

C. Candlestick Patterns

Candlestick patterns are essential tools in price action trading, and some patterns often signal shifts in buyer and seller dominance. Here are a few critical ones:

Doji: This shows indecision in the market. When a doji appears after a strong trend, it might signal a reversal.

Engulfing Pattern: A larger candle that “engulfs” the previous one, signaling a potential reversal in the direction of the larger candle.

Pin Bar: A candle with a long wick (or tail) that shows rejection at certain levels. If it appears in an uptrend or downtrend, it might indicate a reversal.

very important thing is we can’t able to make a complete decision based on one candle we need to check all the previous price action structures before the entry.

4. Analyzing Price Action by Observing Key Elements

A. Market Structure

Market structure refers to the patterns formed by price swings. The primary structures are:

Breakouts: When the price breaks through a support or resistance level, often indicating a potential new trend.

Pullbacks/Retracements: Small reversals in a trend, often providing traders with better entry points.

Swing Highs and Lows: Significant price levels formed as prices create peaks and valleys. By watching these, traders can spot trend strength and potential reversals.

B. Momentum

Momentum measures the strength of a trend. One way traders gauge momentum is by observing the size and speed of price movements. For instance, if an uptrend suddenly shows smaller candlesticks and lower highs, it may suggest fading momentum.

5. Reading Price Action Through Top Traders' Techniques

A. Mark Minervini: Known for his focus on high-momentum stocks, Minervini identifies price patterns in strong uptrends. His approach emphasizes using price action to confirm trends rather than using indicators. By observing how stocks behave near critical levels, he anticipates the "breakout" moments.

B. Paul Tudor Jones: A master of sentiment-driven price action, Jones looks at how price reacts to news and key events. For instance, a stock that rallies after bad news often signals strong underlying demand, which Jones interprets as a bullish signal.

C. Linda Raschke: Specializing in short-term trading, Raschke watches for "false breakouts" and "whipsaws," where prices temporarily break through support or resistance but then return. These false moves often signal larger trends and give opportunities for reversal trades.

6. Common Price Action Trading Strategies

A. Breakout Trading

Breakout trading involves entering a trade when the price breaks out of a support or resistance level. Top traders look for higher volume during breakouts, as this signals conviction in the price movement. It's essential to wait for confirmation — a retest of the breakout level or strong volume — to avoid false breakouts.

B. Reversal Trading

Reversals occur when prices change direction after reaching a significant support or resistance level. Traders look for patterns like double tops/bottoms, head and shoulders, or candlestick signals (e.g., engulfing patterns). The key is to ensure there's a clear trend change before entering the trade.

C. Pullback Trading

In a trending market, pullbacks (temporary price reversals) offer potential entry points. Traders watch for price to pull back to previous support or resistance levels. A well-timed entry during a pullback can offer lower risk, as the trend has already been established.

7. Risk Management in Price Action

Price action trading requires robust risk management:

Stop Losses: Placing stop-loss orders below key support or above key resistance levels can protect against unexpected reversals.

Position Sizing: Adjusting trade size based on the risk involved. Many traders risk only 1-2% of their account per trade.

Trailing Stops: Moving the stop-loss to lock in profits as the trade moves in your favor.

8. The Role of Psychology in Price Action Trading

Understanding price action isn't just about reading charts — it's also about managing emotions:

Patience: Waiting for the right setups rather than forcing trades is crucial. Top traders wait for clear patterns rather than reacting impulsively.

Discipline: Sticking to a plan helps avoid emotional decisions. If a setup doesn't align with your rules, it's better to pass than risk a low-quality trade.

Emotional Detachment: Price action trading can be highly subjective. It's essential to remain objective and avoid "forcing" interpretations onto the market.

9. Practicing Price Action with Backtesting and Real-time Observation

Price action skills improve with experience. Start by backtesting strategies on historical data to understand how they perform in various market conditions. Live observation in demo accounts can also help, allowing you to apply price action concepts without risking real capital. By regularly practicing and refining, traders build the confidence and skills to read the markets effectively.

Summary of Key Points:

Price action is a method of analyzing raw price movements without indicators.

Focus on trends, support/resistance, and key patterns like candlesticks to gain insights into buyer/seller behavior.

Backtesting and practicing with real-time data are essential to building confidence in price action trading.

Embrace risk management and maintain a strong trader mindset to reduce impulsive decisions.

ꕤ

OUR CONTACT LINKS

[**WWW.RETROTRADING.ONLINE**] OUR WEBSITE

RETRO_TRADING_ [INSTA]

[https://www.instagram.com/retro_trading_/profilecard/?igsh=N3hvaWNlbGo4bGd2]

III

Reading Candlesticks and Charts

Candlestick charts are the foundation of price action trading. They provide a snapshot of the emotions, movements, and behavior of buyers and sellers within a certain timeframe. In this chapter, we'll cover the basics of candlestick charts, how to read them, and the types of signals they provide. By the end, you'll be able to interpret charts with confidence and use them to make better trading decisions

What is a Candlestick Chart?

A candlestick chart visually represents price movements over a set time period. Each "candlestick" shows the opening, closing, high, and low prices for a given period (e.g., 1 minute, 1 hour, 1 day). The unique shapes, colors, and patterns of candlesticks reveal market sentiment and momentum, helping traders gauge the direction of price trends.

Structure of a Candlestick

1. Body: Shows the opening and closing prices.

Green/White Body: Closing price is higher than the opening price (bullish).

Red/Black Body: Closing price is lower than the opening price (bearish).

2. Wicks (or Shadows): Lines above and below the body, showing the highest and lowest prices within the time period.

3. Top of the Body (Close/High): The highest price reached if it's a bullish candle; the closing price if bearish.

4. Bottom of the Body (Open/Low): The lowest price if it's bullish; the opening price if bearish.

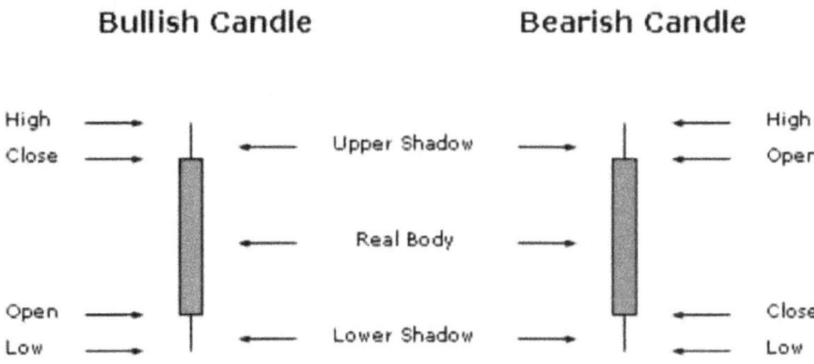

Basic Candlestick Patterns

There are hundreds of candlestick patterns, but here we'll focus on a few essential ones for beginners:

1. Doji

The Doji is a unique pattern where the opening and closing prices are almost identical, creating a thin or non-existent body. It represents indecision in the market, where neither buyers nor sellers have full control. The Doji pattern can lead to reversals or continuation patterns, depending on the surrounding context.

Example: Suppose an uptrend is showing strength, but suddenly, a Doji forms. This could suggest that buyers are losing momentum, and a reversal might be coming. However, wait for confirmation with the next candle.

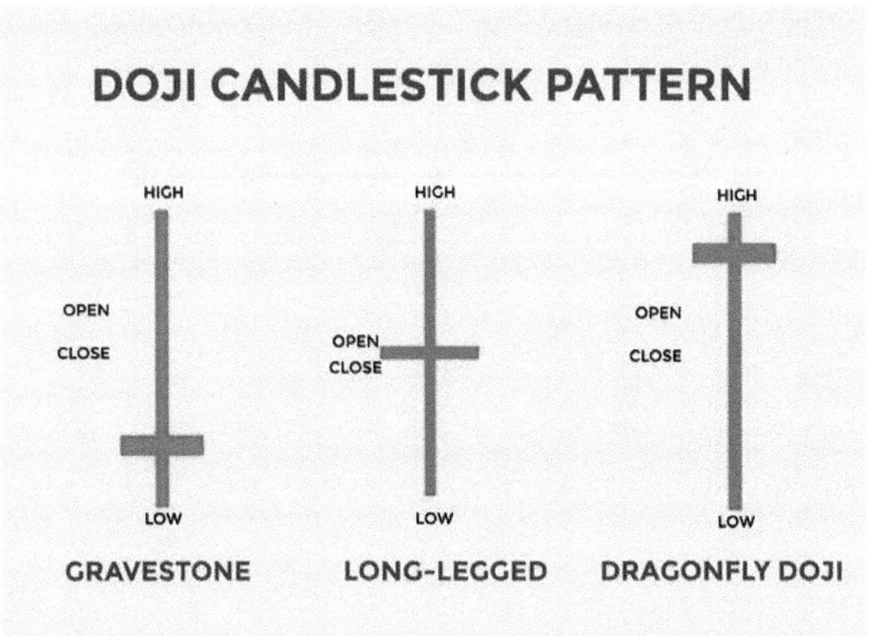

2. Hammer and Inverted Hammer

The Hammer is a bullish reversal pattern often appearing at the end of a downtrend. It has a small body and a long lower shadow, indicating that buyers pushed the price up after a period of selling pressure.

The Inverted Hammer is similar but has a long upper wick. It suggests potential reversal but needs confirmation from subsequent bullish movement.

Example of Hammer: Imagine a stock price falling over several days. A hammer appears, followed by a green (bullish) candle the next day, signaling a possible uptrend.

Example of Inverted Hammer: Suppose a downtrend pauses and an inverted hammer appears, followed by a strong bullish candle. This pattern signals that buyers are potentially gaining control.

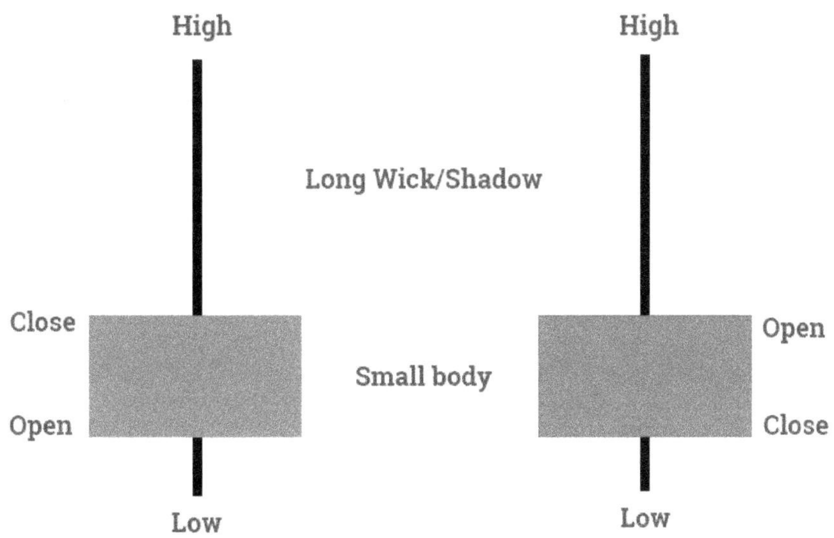

3. Engulfing Patterns

An Engulfing Pattern occurs when a smaller candlestick is followed by a larger candlestick that completely engulfs the previous one. There are two types:

Bullish Engulfing: When a small bearish candle is followed by a larger bullish candle, often suggesting a reversal to the upside.

Bearish Engulfing: When a small bullish candle is engulfed by a larger bearish candle, indicating a potential downside.

Example: In a downtrend, if a bullish engulfing pattern appears near a support level, it could signal an upcoming reversal.

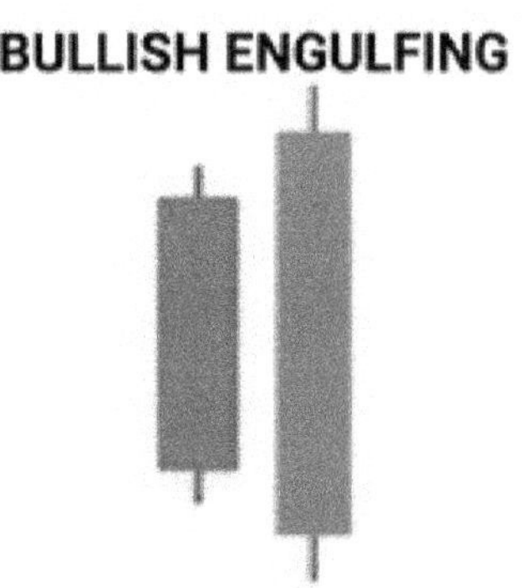

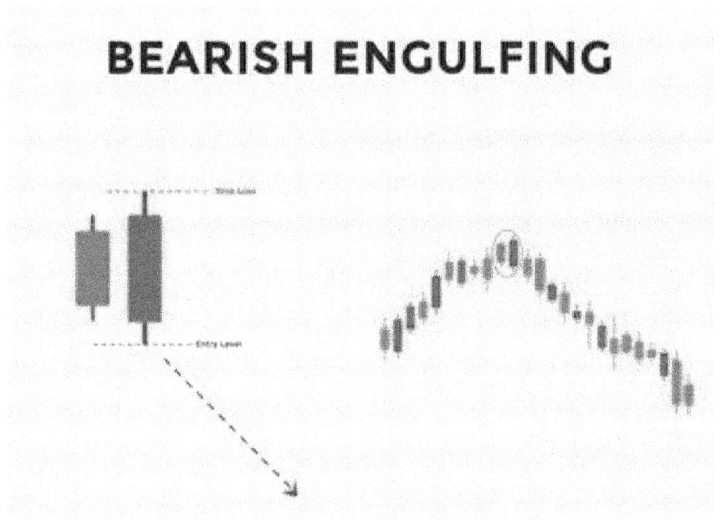

4. Shooting Star

The Shooting Star is a bearish reversal pattern that typically appears at the end of an uptrend. It has a small body, long upper wick, and little or no lower wick, showing that buyers pushed prices up but then sellers regained control.

Example: Suppose a stock is in an uptrend, and a shooting star forms. If the next candle is bearish, it may confirm the beginning of a downtrend, signaling traders to consider selling.

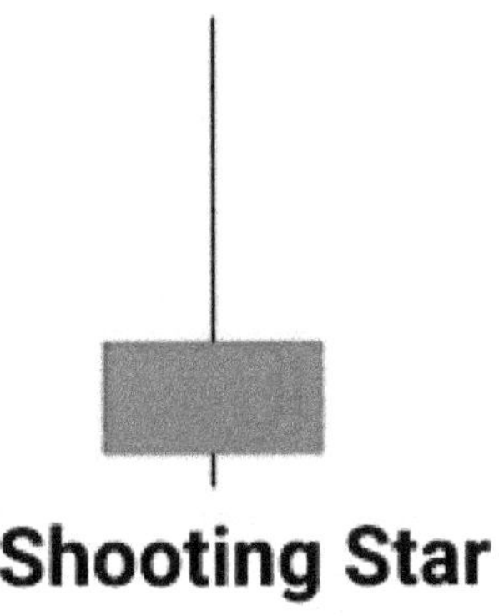

5. Morning Star and Evening Star

These are three-candle patterns that indicate a reversal.

Morning Star: Bullish reversal pattern. It starts with a bearish candle, followed by a small-bodied candle (which could be bearish or bullish), and then a large bullish candle. This pattern suggests the transition from seller dominance to buyer dominance.

Evening Star: Bearish reversal pattern. It starts with a bullish candle, followed by a small-bodied candle, and ends with a large bearish candle, indicating a shift from buyers to sellers.

Example of Morning Star: Suppose a stock is in a downtrend, and you see a bearish candle, followed by a Doji, then a strong bullish candle. This is a Morning Star, suggesting that prices might start to rise.

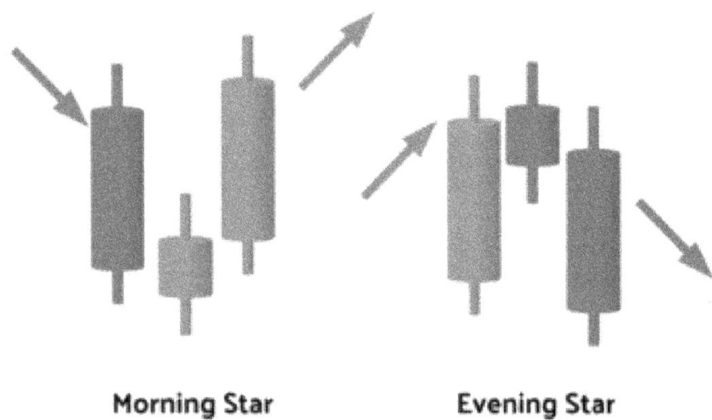

6. Harami Pattern

The Harami Pattern is a two-candle pattern where a large candlestick is followed by a smaller one contained within its body, resembling a "pregnant" shape. It can be a bullish or bearish indicator, depending on the market trend.

Bullish Harami: Appears in a downtrend and suggests a potential reversal to the upside.

Bearish Harami: Appears in an uptrend and suggests a potential reversal to the downside.

Example of Bullish Harami: Imagine a stock declining steadily, then you see a large red candle, followed by a smaller green candle within its range. This could indicate the end of the downtrend.

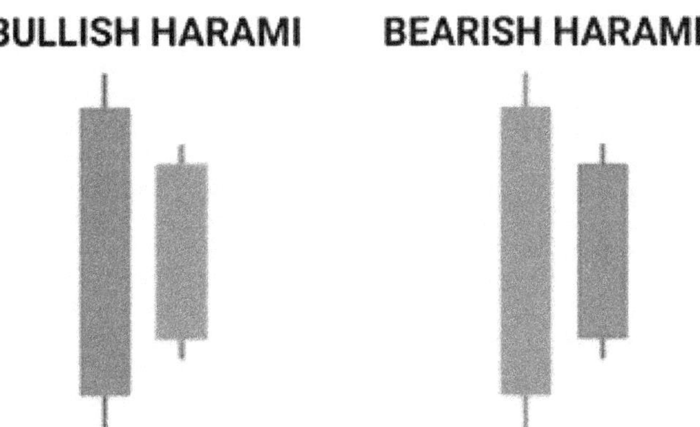

7. Three White Soldiers and Three Black Crows

These patterns consist of three consecutive candles of the same color, signaling trend continuation or reversal.

Three White Soldiers: A bullish pattern where three strong green candles close progressively higher, indicating continued buying momentum and a potential uptrend.

Three Black Crows: A bearish pattern with three red candles closing lower, suggesting strong selling pressure and a potential downtrend.

Example of Three White Soldiers: Suppose a stock is recovering from a pullback, and you see three consecutive bullish candles forming. This shows strong buying momentum, signaling a good opportunity to buy.

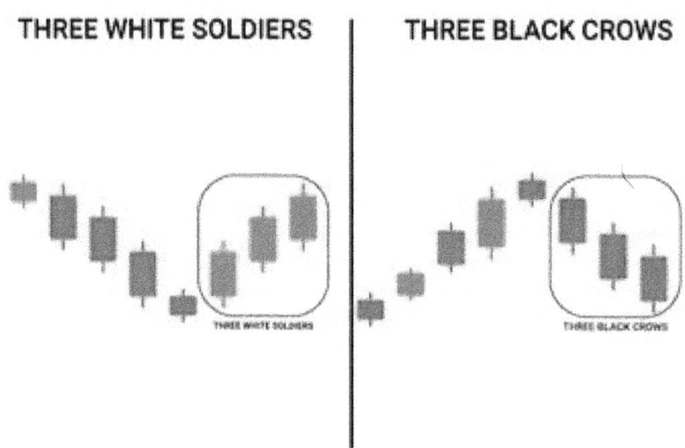

Additional Key Terms and Tips

Support and Resistance Levels: These are horizontal levels on the chart where price historically reverses. Combining candlestick patterns with these levels can enhance the accuracy of trade entries.

Confirmation: Always wait for confirmation of a pattern before acting, such as another candle that aligns with the direction indicated by the pattern.

Volume: High volume on a candlestick pattern increases its reliability. Low volume may lead to false signals.

Chart Example

Imagine you're analyzing a stock with recent market volatility. You notice a Hammer forming after a steep decline, signaling potential buyer interest. After the Hammer, you see a Bullish Engulfing pattern, further supporting a reversal. If this setup appears near a support level, it's even stronger confirmation of a potential entry.

OUR CONTACT LINKS

[**WWW.RETROTRADING.ONLINE**] OUR WEBSITE

RETRO_TRADING_ [INSTA]

[https://www.instagram.com/
retro_trading_/profilecard/?igsh=N3hvaWNlbGo4bGd2]

IV

Support and Resistance Levels

Support and resistance are fundamental concepts in technical analysis, helping traders understand and interpret price movements. These levels act as psychological barriers where prices tend to reverse or experience strong buying/selling pressure. Learning to identify these levels is crucial for making informed trading decisions, whether you're day trading, swing trading, or even investing for the long term.

What is Support?

Support is a price level where a downtrend is expected to pause due to a concentration of buying interest. It acts as a "floor" that prevents prices from falling further as buyers step in. Typically, support levels are created due to historical price action, where the price has bounced off certain levels multiple times.

Example: Imagine a stock price consistently drops to $50 but struggles to fall below it. This $50 level is considered support because buyers tend to enter at this price, pushing the price back up.

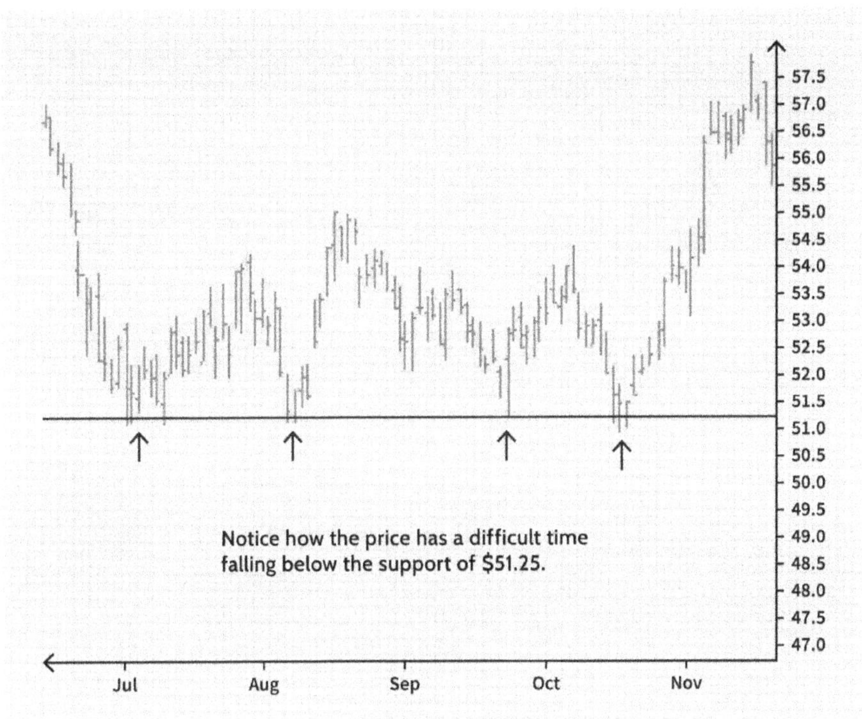

What is Resistance?

Resistance is the opposite of support. It is a price level where an uptrend is expected to pause due to selling interest. This level acts as a "ceiling" that prevents prices from rising higher as sellers step in, taking profits or short-selling.

Example: If a stock's price consistently rises to $100 but fails to break above this level, $100 is considered a resistance level. Sellers come in at this point, leading to a price drop each time it reaches this level.

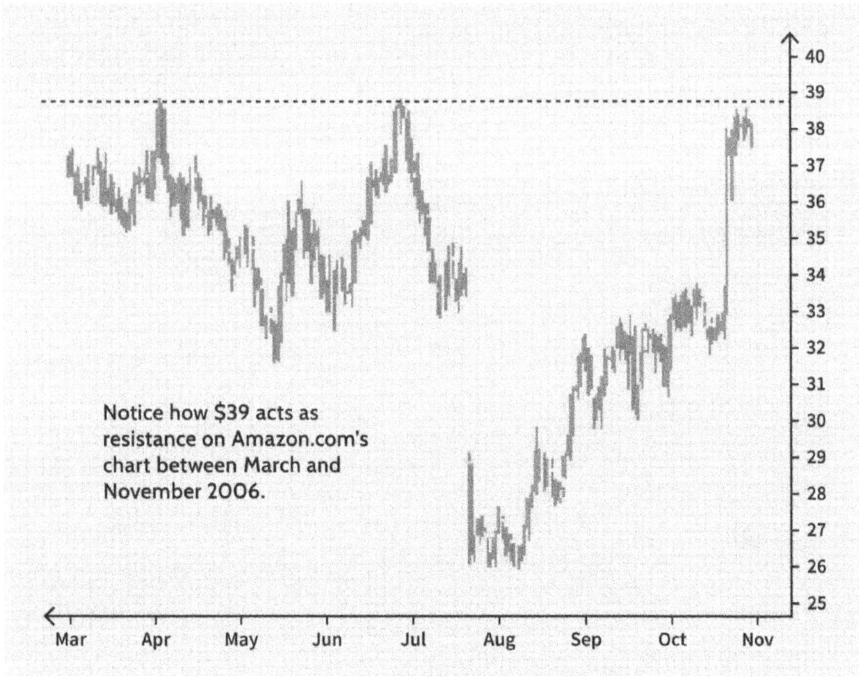

Why are Support and Resistance Levels Important?

Support and resistance levels are crucial for traders because they help identify potential entry and exit points. By observing how price behaves around these levels, traders can anticipate possible reversals, breakouts, or even consolidations, allowing them to make more strategic decisions.

Key Takeaway: Buying near support and selling near resistance is a common strategy. However, waiting for confirmation of these levels can increase accuracy and reduce the chances of false signals.

Types of Support and Resistance

1. Horizontal Support and Resistance

These levels are drawn across previous highs and lows where price has reversed multiple times. They are considered some of the strongest and most reliable levels.

Example: If a stock price hits $200 three times and drops back, $200 becomes a horizontal resistance level.

2. Trendline Support and Resistance

Trendlines are diagonal lines drawn along successive highs or lows. They act as dynamic support or resistance levels in trending markets.

Example: In an uptrend, a line drawn connecting the recent higher lows can serve as a trendline support. The price will likely find support along this line

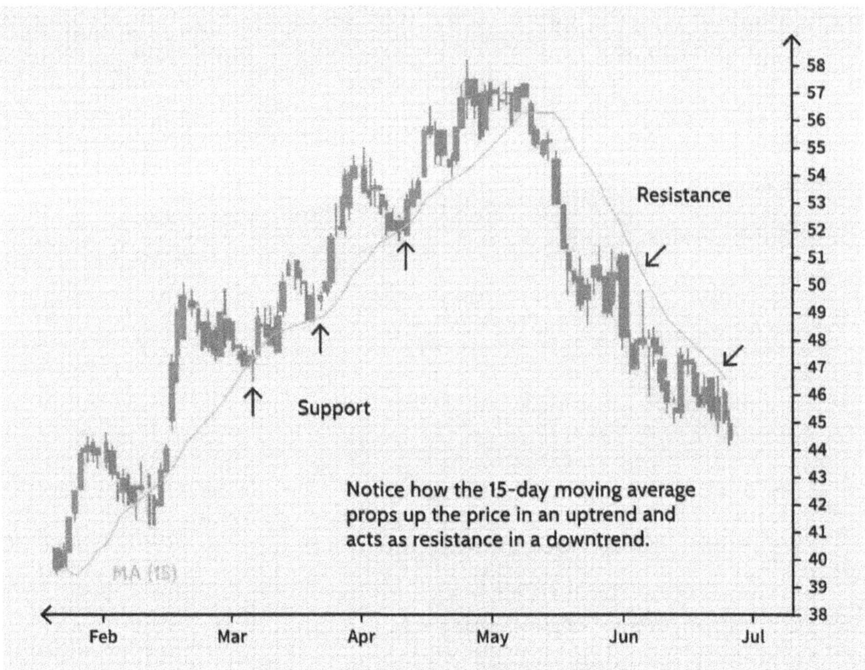

3. Moving Averages as Support and Resistance

Moving averages like the 50-day and 200-day are often used as dynamic support and resistance levels. When the price is above a moving average, it may act as support, and when below, it can act as resistance.

Example: If a stock is trading above its 50-day moving average, this average may act as a support level. When it moves below, the average may act as a resistance level.

4. Fibonacci Levels

Fibonacci retracement levels, such as 38.2%, 50%, and 61.8%, often act as support and resistance in a trend. These levels are derived from the Fibonacci sequence and are popular for identifying potential reversal areas.

Example: In an uptrend, the price might retrace to the 38.2% level, where it finds support before continuing upward.

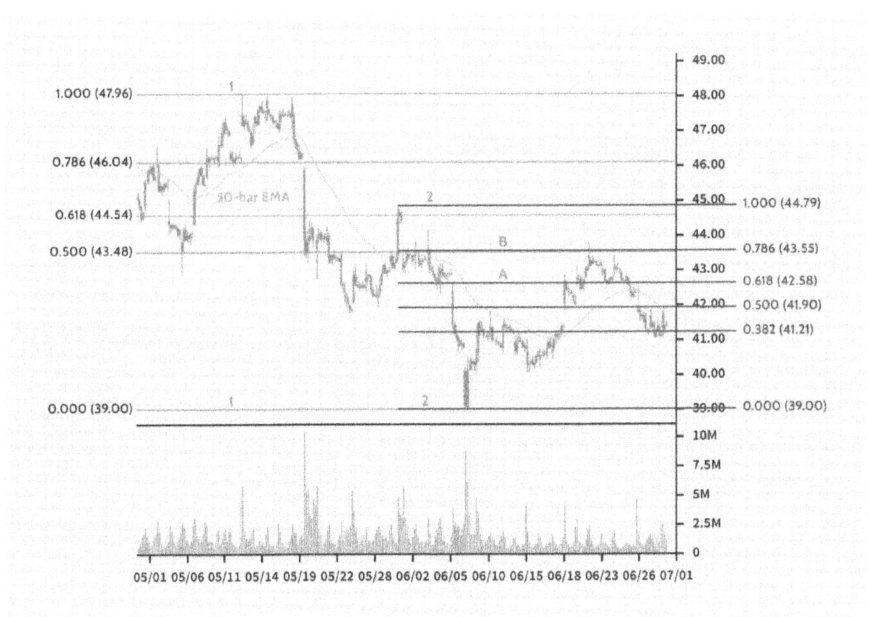

How to Identify Support and Resistance

1. Price Action Analysis

Analyzing historical price movements helps determine key levels where price has reversed multiple times. These areas are potential support or resistance levels.

Example: If a stock reversed from $90 twice in the past, $90 could be considered a support level.

2. Volume Analysis

Volume can indicate the strength of a support or resistance level. High trading volume at a level implies stronger support or resistance because it represents significant buying or selling interest.

Example: If a stock approaches a resistance level with high volume but fails to break through, it confirms the strength of that resistance.

3. Using Technical Indicators

Indicators like RSI, MACD, and Bollinger Bands can help identify overbought or oversold conditions around support and resistance levels, signaling potential reversals.

Example: When RSI is overbought near resistance, a reversal to the downside might be imminent.

Support and Resistance in Different Market Phases

1. Trending Markets

In an uptrend, resistance levels may turn into support if the price breaks through and holds above them. This is known as a support-resistance flip.

Example: A stock breaks through $120 resistance, then pulls back to $120, which now acts as a support level.

2. Range-Bound Markets

In a range-bound market, price bounces between established support and resistance levels, offering multiple trading opportunities within this range.

Example: If a stock oscillates between $100 and $120, traders can buy near $100 and sell near $120 until a breakout occurs.

3. Breakout and Breakdown Scenarios

When the price breaks above a resistance or below a support level with strong momentum, it's known as a breakout (upward) or breakdown (downward). Breakouts often lead to significant price movements.

Example: A stock breaks above $150 resistance with strong volume, indicating an uptrend may continue.

Common Mistakes with Support and Resistance

1. Relying on Support and Resistance Alone

Support and resistance should not be used in isolation. Combining them with other tools, like trendlines and technical indicators, improves accuracy.

2. Ignoring Volume

Volume is essential for confirming breakouts or breakdowns. Low-volume breakouts may fail and result in "false breakouts."

3. Setting Rigid Levels

Support and resistance are not exact prices but zones. Prices may fluctuate slightly above or below these levels, so it's important to allow for a margin of error.

Final Thoughts: Mastering Support and Resistance

Support and resistance are crucial to reading price action and understanding market sentiment. Recognizing these levels can improve your timing, increase your confidence in entries and exits, and ultimately help you make more informed trading decisions. As with any trading strategy, practice and experience are essential to mastering the art of interpreting support and resistance. By combining these levels with indicators and proper risk management, you can navigate the markets more effectively.

ꙮ

OUR CONTACT LINKS

[**WWW.RETROTRADING.ONLINE**] OUR WEBSITE

RETRO_TRADING_ [INSTA]

[https://www.instagram.com/retro_trading_/profilecard/?igsh=N3hvaWNlbGo4bGd2]

V

Trends and Trendlines

In trading, identifying trends and understanding trendlines is fundamental for analyzing price movement and predicting market behavior. This chapter dives into the essential concepts of trends and trendlines, including how to identify different types of trends, the importance of trendlines in technical analysis, and ways to effectively use trendlines in your trading strategy. Whether you're a beginner or an intermediate trader, mastering these concepts will give you an edge in anticipating price direction.

What is a Trend?

A trend represents the general direction in which a market or asset's price is moving over time. Trends reflect the market sentiment—whether buyers (bulls) or sellers (bears) are dominating. In general, a trend can be upward (bullish), downward (bearish), or sideways (consolidating). Recognizing the direction of a trend is crucial, as "the trend is your friend" is a well-known trading maxim that highlights the importance of aligning with the current trend.

Example: In a bullish trend, a stock might move from $50 to $100 over several months, with higher highs and higher lows along the way.

Types of Trends

1. Uptrend (Bullish Trend):

An uptrend occurs when prices consistently make higher highs and higher lows. It reflects strong buying interest and positive sentiment about the asset.

Characteristics: Higher highs and higher lows.

Example: Apple Inc. (AAPL) often shows uptrends during positive earnings seasons, where prices gradually increase over weeks or months.

2. Downtrend (Bearish Trend):

A downtrend is marked by lower highs and lower lows, signaling persistent selling pressure and negative sentiment.

Characteristics: Lower highs and lower lows.

Example: During the 2008 financial crisis, many assets showed strong downtrends as investor sentiment plummeted.

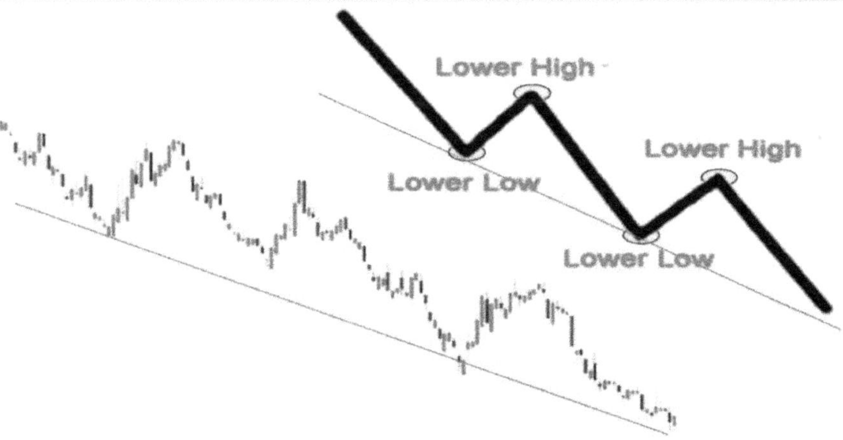

3. Sideways Trend (Consolidation):

In a sideways trend, prices fluctuate within a narrow range, showing no clear direction. This phase often reflects market indecision or a pause before the next major move.

Characteristics: Price oscillates between support and resistance levels without breaking out.

Example: Bitcoin often consolidates in sideways trends for weeks before making a major upward or downward movement.

What is a Trendline?

A trendline is a straight line that connects two or more price points on a chart, providing a visual representation of the trend. Trendlines help identify areas of support in an uptrend and resistance in a downtrend, which traders use to determine potential entry and exit points.

1. Uptrend Line:

In an uptrend, trendlines are drawn by connecting the lows of the trend. This line acts as support, and the price typically bounces off it during corrections within the trend.

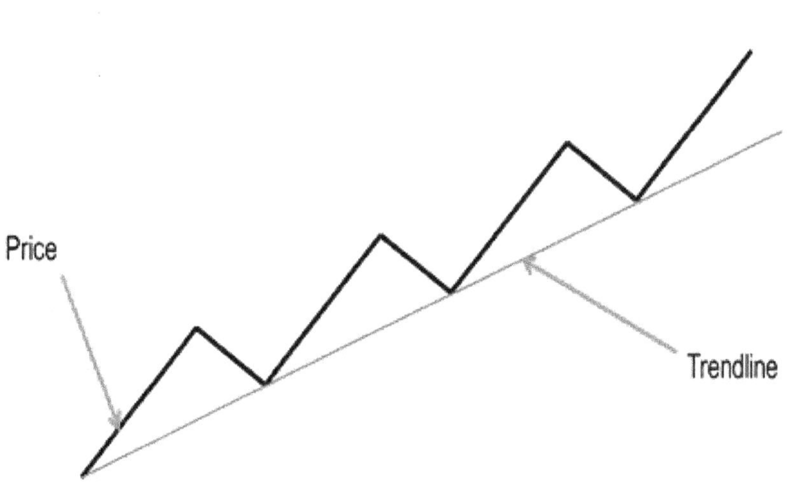

2. Downtrend Line:

In a downtrend, trendlines are drawn by connecting the highs of the trend. This line acts as resistance, and prices often fail to break above it, resuming the downtrend.

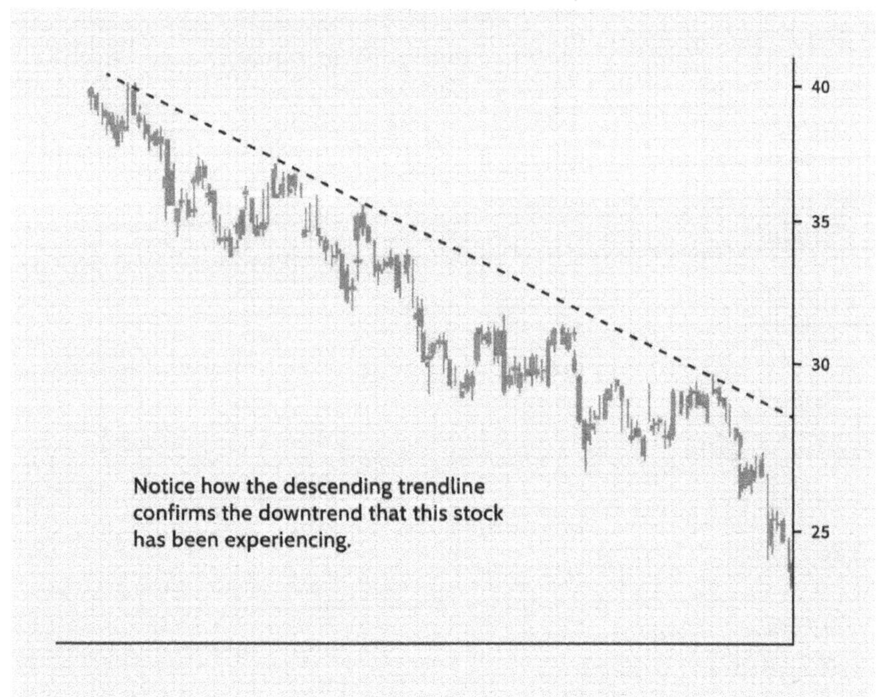

Drawing Trendlines

1. Identify the Trend: First, determine the general direction of the price movement.

2. Select Two Major Points: For an uptrend, pick two significant lows; for a downtrend, select two significant highs.

3. Extend the Line: Extend the trendline beyond the two points. This line acts as a guide for future price action.

Important Tips:

Use higher timeframes for stronger, more reliable trendlines.

Avoid forcing a trendline to fit. The line should connect natural highs or lows without cutting through price candles.

Using Trendlines in Trading

1. Trendline Breakouts:

When price breaks through a trendline, it often signals a potential trend reversal. This can be a powerful indicator, especially if confirmed with high trading volume.

Example: If a downtrend line is broken, it might signal the beginning of a bullish reversal, and traders might consider entering long positions.

2. Using Trendlines as Support and Resistance:

Trendlines act as dynamic support and resistance levels. In an uptrend, the trendline provides support where traders may look for buying opportunities. In a downtrend, the trendline serves as resistance for potential short trades.

Example: In an uptrend, traders could place buy orders near the trendline, expecting the price to bounce and continue upward.

3. Multiple Timeframes:

Analyzing trendlines on multiple timeframes can provide a broader perspective on price movement. A trendline on a daily chart may give insight into a long-term trend, while a trendline on a 15-minute chart shows short-term market behavior.

Example: A trader might look for alignment between an uptrend on a weekly chart and an uptrend on a daily chart to confirm a long-term bullish outlook.

Trendline Trading Strategies

1. Bounce Strategy:

This involves entering trades when the price "bounces" off a trendline. In an uptrend, buy when the price touches the trendline; in a downtrend, sell short when it touches the trendline.

Example: If a stock is in an uptrend, a trader could buy when the price bounces off the trendline, expecting the upward momentum to continue.

2. Breakout Strategy:

Entering a trade after a trendline is broken can signal a potential reversal. Traders wait for the price to break the trendline and often use confirmation indicators (like volume) before entering.

Example: If a downtrend line is broken and volume increases, it can indicate a reversal, prompting traders to consider a buy position.

3. Pullback to Trendline:

After a trendline breakout, prices often "pull back" to the trendline before resuming the new trend. Traders can wait for this pullback to confirm the trend change.

Example: When a downtrend line is broken, the price may pull back to test it as support before moving higher. This is a potential entry point for a long position.

Common Mistakes with Trendlines

1. Overfitting Trendlines:

Trendlines should not be forced to fit every movement in price. Overfitting can result in unreliable signals. Use significant highs or lows and avoid adjusting the trendline to fit minor price fluctuations.

2. Ignoring Volume:

Volume plays a crucial role in confirming trendline breakouts. Low volume can lead to false breakouts, while high volume provides confirmation.

3. Relying Solely on Trendlines:

Trendlines are effective tools but should be combined with other forms of analysis. Relying solely on trendlines can lead to missed signals or false assumptions.

Final Thoughts: Mastering Trends and Trendlines

Trends and trendlines are among the most reliable tools in a trader's toolkit. Understanding how to draw and interpret them can provide a clearer picture of market sentiment, helping you align your trades with the direction of the trend. Practice identifying trends and drawing trendlines on historical data to improve your skills. Remember, a trendline is only as strong as the trader's discipline in combining it with sound strategy and risk management.

By understanding and applying these techniques, you'll be better equipped to anticipate market movements and make more strategic trading decisions. Let the trends be your guide, but always be prepared for changes, as markets are constantly evolving.

ꕥ

VI

Mastering Chart Patterns

Chart patterns are essential tools in technical analysis, helping traders predict future price movements by studying historical price behavior. By recognizing patterns, traders can identify potential points of continuation or reversal in a market, which can be pivotal in making strategic trading decisions. This chapter will cover some of the most commonly observed chart patterns, breaking down their components, the psychology behind them, and how traders can use them effectively.

What Are Chart Patterns?

Chart patterns are specific formations created by price movements on a chart. They are classified into two major types:

1. Reversal Patterns: These indicate that a trend may be coming to an end, potentially leading to a trend reversal.

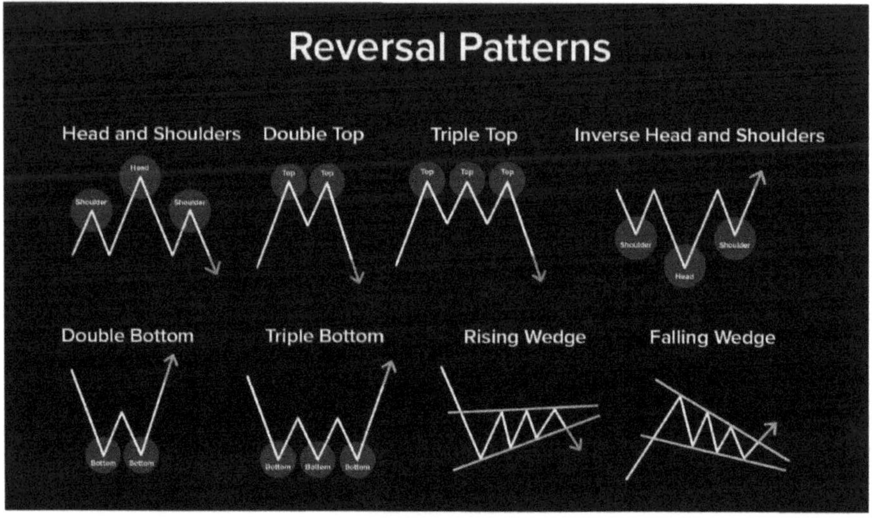

2. Continuation Patterns: These suggest that the trend will likely continue in the same direction after a brief consolidation.

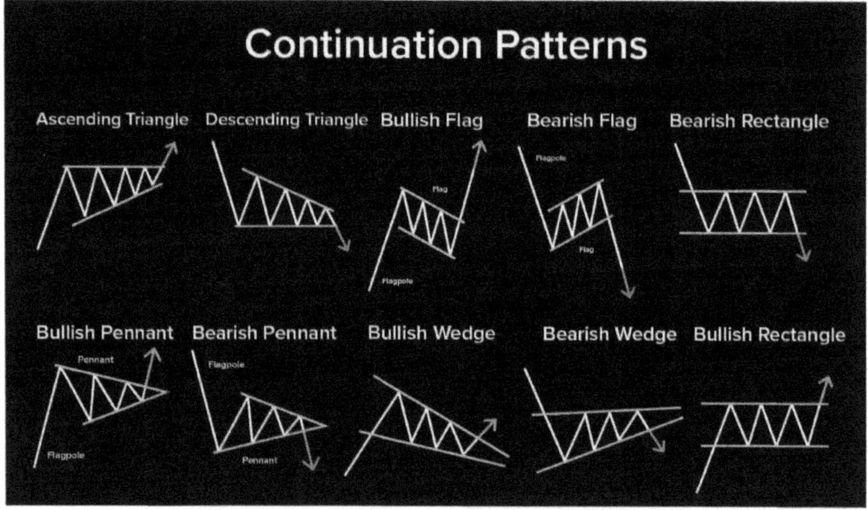

Recognizing chart patterns can provide traders with actionable insights and can be used in conjunction with other indicators like volume and trendlines.

Key Reversal Patterns

1. Head and Shoulders

The head and shoulders pattern signals a potential reversal from an uptrend to a downtrend. This pattern consists of three peaks: a larger middle peak (the head) flanked by two smaller peaks (the shoulders). A neckline connects the lows of the two shoulders and serves as a crucial support line.

Psychology: The formation of the first shoulder shows initial buying pressure, but after forming the head, sellers start taking control. When the second shoulder forms and breaks the neckline, it indicates a potential trend reversal.

Example: During an uptrend in Tesla stock, a head and shoulders pattern may indicate that bullish momentum is slowing down, warning traders of an impending downtrend.

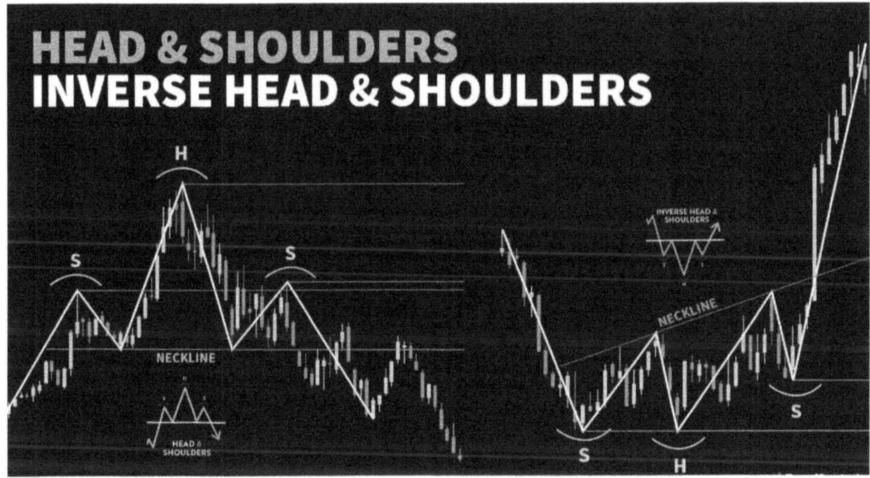

2. Inverse Head and Shoulders

The inverse head and shoulders is the opposite of the head and shoulders, appearing at the end of a downtrend and signaling a potential uptrend reversal.

Psychology: After forming the left shoulder, the sellers push lower but are followed by strong buying interest that forms the head. The formation of the right shoulder and a break above the neckline can confirm the reversal.

Example: In Bitcoin's 2018 bear market, an inverse head and shoulders pattern signaled the end of the downtrend and the beginning of a new bullish cycle.

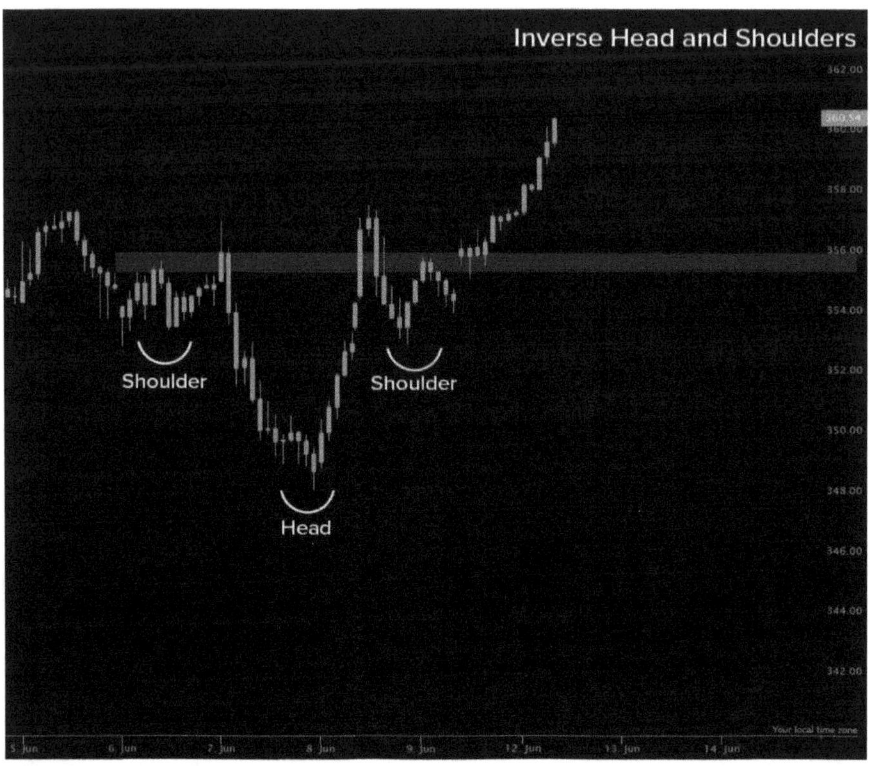

3. Double Top and Double Bottom

Double Top: This pattern appears at the end of an uptrend and signals a potential reversal. It consists of two peaks at roughly the same price level, with a trough in between.

Psychology: After the first peak, sellers gain control, and the price drops. When buyers attempt to push prices up again, they fail to surpass the first peak, signaling exhaustion.

Example: Apple stock in 2021 showed a double top, suggesting the uptrend was losing steam.

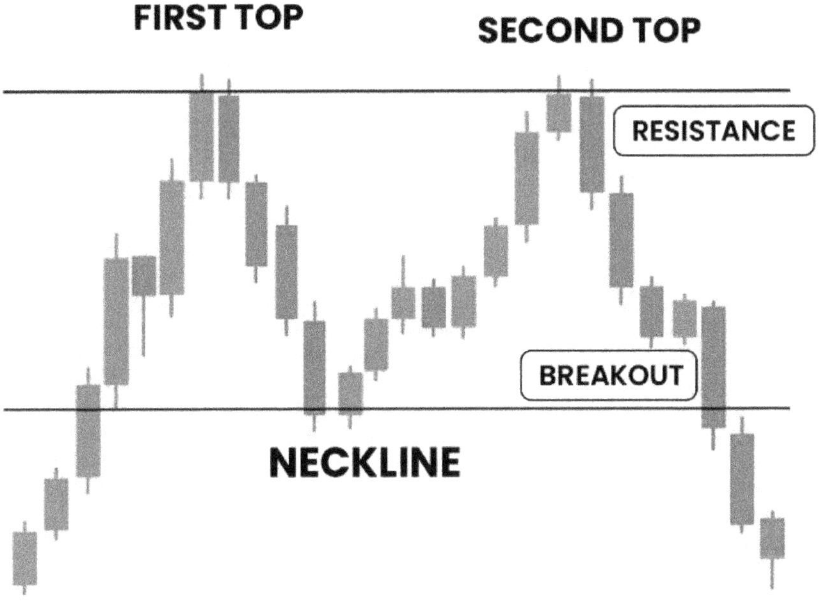

Double Bottom: This occurs at the end of a downtrend, showing two troughs at the same price level, separated by a peak.

Psychology: After the first trough, buyers attempt to push prices up, but sellers take control again. However, when prices reach the previous low, buyers re-enter, creating a reversal.

Example: Ethereum in early 2020 showed a double bottom before rallying.

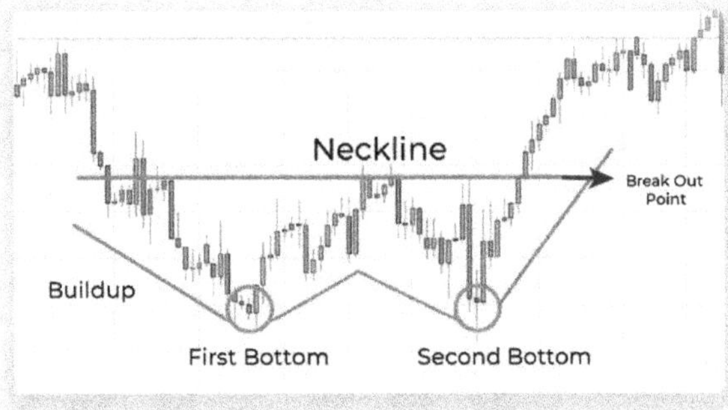

Key Continuation Patterns

1. Flags and Pennants

Flags and pennants indicate a continuation in the current trend after a period of consolidation. They are characterized by a sharp price move (flagpole), followed by a consolidation phase.

Flag: A rectangular, parallel channel sloping against the trend.

Psychology: After a strong trend move, traders take profits, resulting in a consolidation. When the breakout occurs, it often resumes the initial trend with renewed strength.

Example: Tesla's stock showed flag patterns repeatedly in 2020's bullish rally, indicating brief consolidations before continued upward moves.

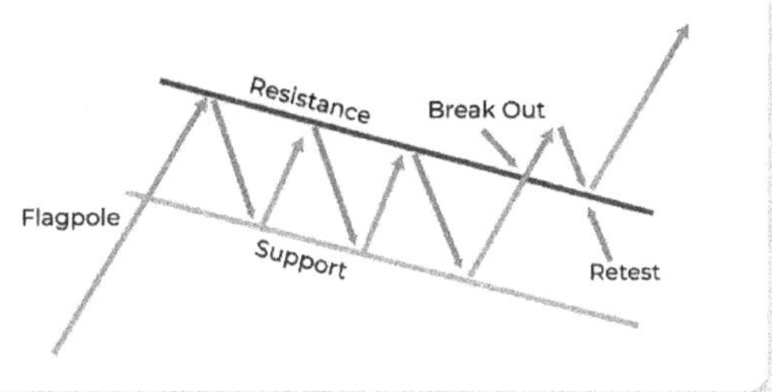

Pennant: A small symmetrical triangle after a sharp move.

Psychology: Similar to flags, pennants form as traders pause after a strong trend. The breakout direction typically follows the initial trend.

Example: Pennants are often seen in volatile assets like crude oil after strong directional moves.

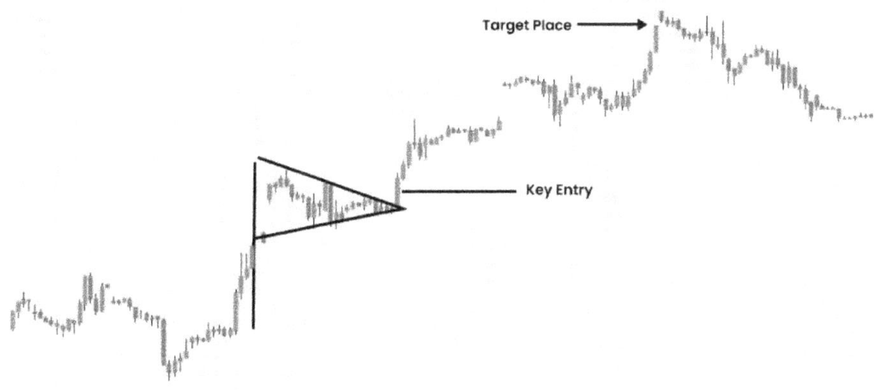

Enter Caption

2. Triangles

Triangles are versatile patterns that can signal both continuation and reversal. There are three types: ascending, descending, and symmetrical.

Ascending Triangle: Formed by a horizontal resistance line and an upward-sloping support line.

Psychology: Buyers gradually push prices higher, and a breakout above resistance indicates strong bullish interest.

Example: An ascending triangle in the S&P 500 often signals a bullish breakout.

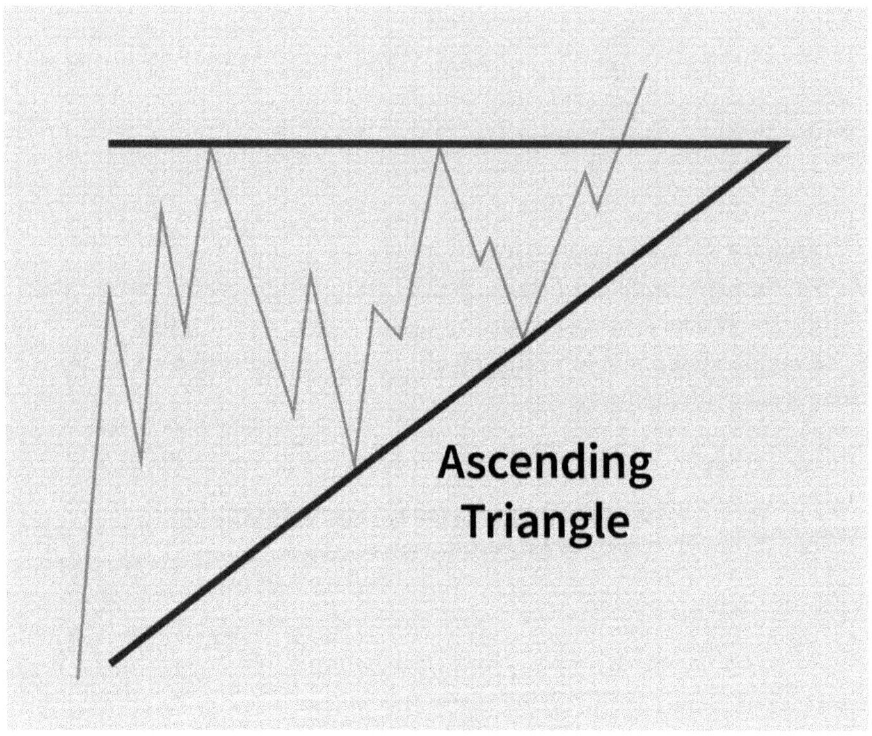

Descending Triangle: Created by a horizontal support line and a downward-sloping resistance line.

Psychology: Sellers push prices lower, and a breakdown below support shows increasing bearish sentiment.

Example: A descending triangle in a cryptocurrency pair may signal a breakdown and further downside.

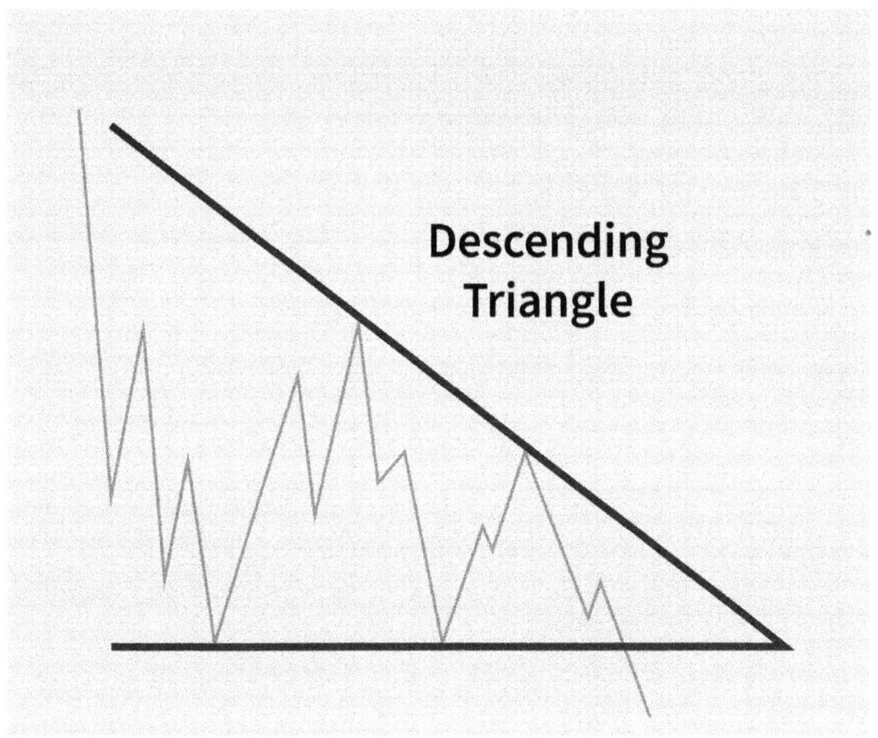

Symmetrical Triangle: Both resistance and support lines converge, creating a triangle shape.

Psychology: Price consolidates, with neither buyers nor sellers dominating. A breakout in either direction can signal the trend continuation.

Example: Symmetrical triangles in forex markets show periods of indecision before major trend continuations.

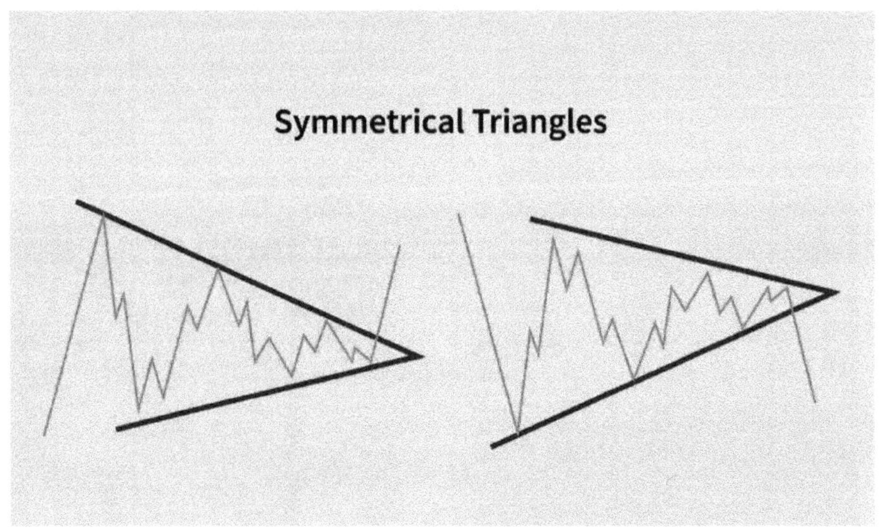

3. Wedges

Wedges are similar to triangles but are generally steeper and can signal reversals.

Rising Wedge: A bearish pattern in an uptrend, where price consolidates in an upward-sloping, narrowing range.

Psychology: Although prices are moving up, the slowing momentum suggests weakening buyer strength, indicating a potential reversal.

Example: A rising wedge in the tech sector could signal a pullback after an extensive rally.

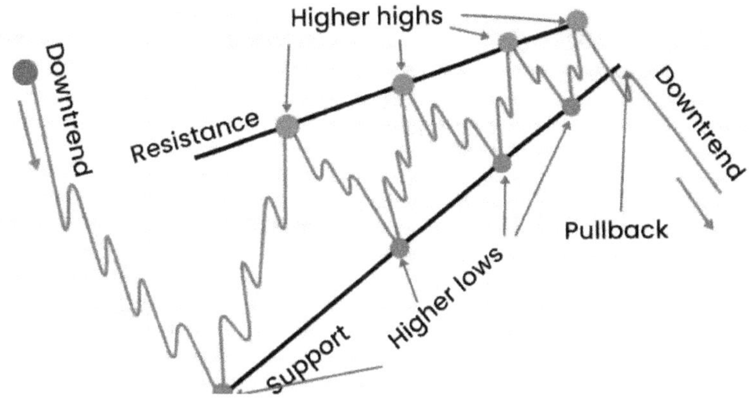

Falling Wedge: A bullish pattern during a downtrend, where price consolidates in a downward-sloping, narrowing range.

Psychology: As sellers lose strength, buyers gradually gain control, leading to a potential breakout.

Example: The SPY ETF has shown falling wedges before reversing to bullish trends during market recoveries.

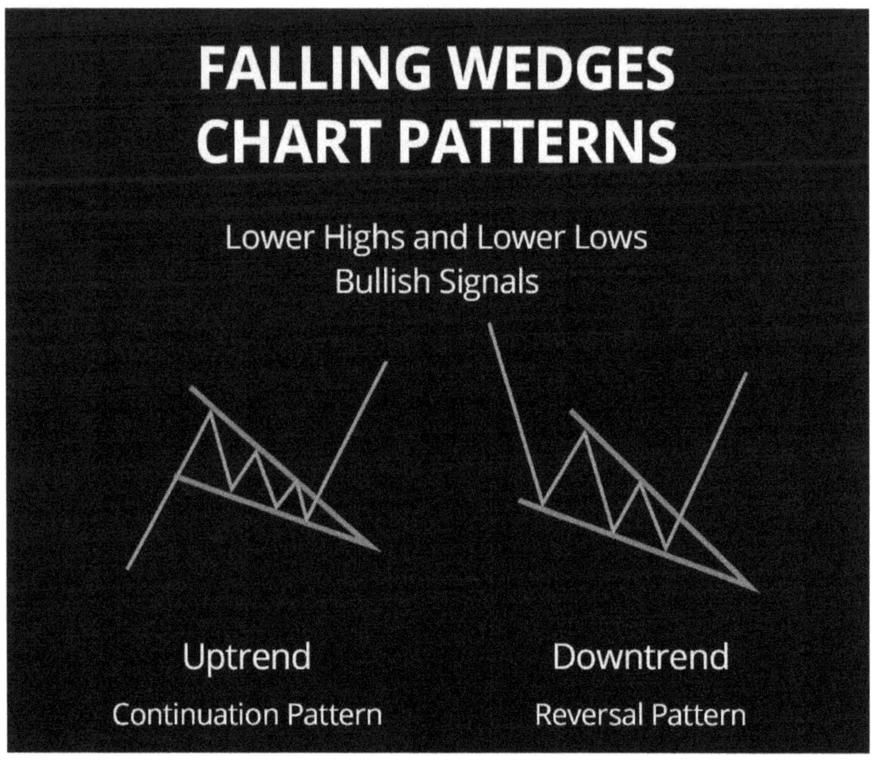

Using Chart Patterns in Trading

1. Confirmation and Volume: Patterns alone are not sufficient; volume helps confirm the pattern's validity. For example, high volume in a breakout from a triangle strengthens the case for continuation.

2. Multiple Timeframes: Observing patterns on multiple timeframes gives a more reliable signal. A pattern confirmed on a daily and weekly chart holds more significance than one on a 5-minute chart.

3. Risk Management: Patterns can guide entries, but it's crucial to use stop-losses to manage risk. For example, place a stop-loss just below the neckline in a head and shoulders pattern.

4. Combining with Indicators: To enhance chart pattern analysis, combine with indicators like RSI for overbought/oversold conditions or MACD for

trend confirmation.

Common Mistakes in Chart Patterns

1. Forcing Patterns: Don't force a pattern to fit. Only trade clear, well-defined patterns.

2. Ignoring Volume: Volume is crucial, especially in breakouts.

3. Entering Without Confirmation: Wait for clear confirmation, like a close above/below a key level, before trading.

Mastering chart patterns can significantly enhance your trading performance. Whether you're spotting reversals with double tops or looking for continuations with flags, these patterns reveal crucial market psychology. By combining them with sound strategy, proper risk management, and practice, chart patterns can provide an invaluable edge in trading.

OUR CONTACT LINKS

[**WWW.RETROTRADING.ONLINE**] OUR WEBSITE

RETRO_TRADING_ [INSTA]

[https://www.instagram.com/retro_trading_/profilecard/?igsh=N3hvaWNlbGo4bGd2]

VII

Entry and Exit Strategies

One of the most critical aspects of trading is knowing when to enter and when to exit a trade. While technical analysis, chart patterns, and fundamental factors can provide insights into market movements, it's the entry and exit strategies that turn those insights into actionable decisions. Without well-planned strategies, even the best analysis can fall short. In this chapter, we'll explore a variety of entry and exit strategies that traders at any level can apply, offering real-world examples to ensure a comprehensive understanding

Understanding Entry Strategies

An entry strategy is a set of guidelines that a trader uses to decide when to open a position. The goal of any entry strategy is to align with the market trend and take advantage of favorable price movements.

1. Breakout Entry Strategy

The breakout strategy is one of the most widely used methods, especially for trend-following traders. Breakouts occur when the price breaks above a resistance level or below a support level, often signaling the start of a new trend.

Steps to Execute:

Identify a strong support or resistance level on the chart.

Wait for the price to break above (for a bullish trade) or below (for a bearish trade) this level.

Confirm the breakout with indicators like volume, as higher volume strengthens the breakout signal.

Example: Suppose Tesla stock has been consolidating at $200, forming a strong resistance level. A breakout above $200 with increased volume might signal a new uptrend, providing an entry point.

Pullback Entry Strategy

A pullback strategy involves entering a trade after the price temporarily moves against the trend, offering an opportunity to join the trend at a better price.

Steps to Execute:

Identify a trend (uptrend for a buy setup, downtrend for a sell setup).

Wait for the price to pull back to a support level (in an uptrend) or resistance level (in a downtrend).

Confirm the setup with indicators like moving averages or RSI.

Example: Apple's stock is in an uptrend, but it pulls back to its 50-day moving average. A bounce from this level can be a signal to enter a long position

Moving Average Crossover Strategy

Moving average crossovers are powerful tools for identifying changes in trend direction and can help traders with entry timing.

Steps to Execute:

Use two moving averages (e.g., 50-day and 200-day).

A bullish crossover occurs when the shorter moving average (50-day) crosses above the longer moving average (200-day).

Enter the trade upon the crossover, aligning with the trend change.

Example: In a forex pair like EUR/USD, a 50-day moving average crossing above the 200-day moving average can suggest an uptrend, providing a potential buy entry.

Candlestick Patterns as Entry Signals

Candlestick patterns like the hammer, engulfing, and doji can serve as entry signals. They provide visual insights into market psychology, indicating shifts in buying or selling momentum.

Example: After a downtrend in crude oil prices, a hammer candlestick forms, showing rejection at a key support level. This can signal a potential reversal, providing an entry point for a long position.

Understanding Exit Strategies

An effective exit strategy protects profits, limits losses, and ensures that you leave a trade at the most opportune moment.

1. Profit Target Exit

Setting a profit target is one of the simplest exit strategies. This is the price level at which you're willing to close a trade and take profits.

Steps to Execute

Define a realistic profit target based on support and resistance levels, Fibonacci retracements, or previous price highs/lows.

Place a take-profit order at this level.

Adjust the profit target if the trend strengthens or additional patterns develop.

Example: If you enter a position at $100 in a stock, you may set a profit target of $110 based on resistance levels. If the stock reaches $110, you close the position.

2. Trailing Stop-Loss

A trailing stop-loss moves along with the price in a favorable direction, helping you secure profits while staying in the trade if the trend continues.

Steps to Execute

Set an initial stop-loss (e.g., 2% below the entry price).

Adjust the stop-loss as the price moves in your favor (e.g., 2% below the highest price reached).

If the price reverses and hits the trailing stop, close the position.

Example: You buy a stock at $50, and the price moves to $55. With a 2% trailing stop, your stop-loss would now be $53.90, securing profits if the stock declines from its peak.

3. Moving Average Exit Strategy

Using a moving average as an exit can help you stay in the trend until it shows signs of reversal.

Steps to Execute:

Use a moving average like the 20-day EMA as a trailing exit.

As long as the price remains above the moving average (for a long trade), stay in the trade.

Exit when the price closes below the moving average.

Example: In a Bitcoin trade, if the price closes below the 20-day EMA, it might signal a weakening trend, indicating an exit.

4. Risk-Reward Ratio Strategy

Establishing a risk-reward ratio ensures that you only enter trades where potential profits are significantly higher than potential losses.

Steps to Execute

Calculate the risk (difference between entry and stop-loss levels).

Set a profit target that is at least 2-3 times the risk.

Exit when the profit target is reached or adjust the stop-loss to break even.

Example: In a forex trade, if your stop-loss is 30 pips, you set a profit target 90 pips away to ensure a 3:1 risk-reward ratio.

Combining Entry and Exit Strategies for Optimal Results

Aligning Entry with Exit Goals: If you're using a breakout entry strategy, consider a trailing stop to capture profits as the trend unfolds.

Risk Management: Never risk more than you can afford to lose. Position sizing and stop-loss orders are crucial.

Patience and Discipline: Stick to your strategy and avoid making impulsive decisions based on market noise or emotions.

Real-World Example: Applying an Entry and Exit Strategy in the Stock Market

Imagine you're trading Amazon stock

Step 1: Entry – You notice a breakout from a long-term resistance level at $3,000 with high volume. Based on the breakout strategy, you decide to enter at $3,000.

Step 2: Setting Stop-Loss and Take-Profit – You place a stop-loss at $2,850 (5% below entry) and set a profit target at $3,600 (20% above entry).

Step 3: Adjusting as Needed – As Amazon rises to $3,400, you implement a trailing stop of 5%, allowing for profit capture if a pullback occurs.

Outcome – Amazon reaches $3,600, and you close the trade, achieving your profit target.

Common Mistakes in Entry and Exit Strategies

Entering Trades Without a Plan: Avoid impulsive entries based on fear of missing out (FOMO).

Overusing Trailing Stops: Trailing stops can be effective but overusing them may lead to premature exits.

Ignoring Market Conditions: Adjust strategies in volatile markets to accommodate higher fluctuations.

Conclusion

Entry and exit strategies form the backbone of a sound trading plan. By thoughtfully combining these strategies, traders can maximize profits, manage risk effectively, and remain disciplined in all market conditions. Whether you're using breakouts, moving averages, or trailing stops, the key is consistency and adaptation to changing market dynamics.

The art of entering and exiting trades goes beyond simple mechanics; it requires understanding market psychology, staying disciplined, and constantly refining your approach. In the following chapters, we'll explore more about trade management and risk mitigation, ensuring a comprehensive skill set for success in trading.

ꕥ

OUR CONTACT LINKS

[**WWW.RETROTRADING.ONLINE**] OUR WEBSITE

RETRO_TRADING_ [INSTA]

[https://www.instagram.com/
retro_trading_/profilecard/?igsh=N3hvaWNlbGo4bGd2]

VIII

Risk Management Essentials

In the world of trading, risk management is the cornerstone that separates successful traders from those who succumb to losses. It's the systematic approach to preserving capital, managing potential losses, and ensuring that one profitable trade doesn't get wiped out by a string of losses. This chapter delves deep into the strategies and principles of risk management, guiding traders of all levels to understand, manage, and mitigate risks effectively.

What is Risk Management?

Risk management is the process of identifying, assessing, and controlling the potential losses in trading. While it's natural to focus on profits, sustainable trading success comes from an equal—if not greater—focus on controlling losses. Proper risk management allows traders to withstand inevitable losing trades and helps them remain in the market long enough to realize gains from winning trades.

Why is Risk Management Important?

The volatile nature of markets means that even well-informed trades can go against expectations. No one can predict every market move accurately, so the aim isn't to avoid losses altogether but to limit them and protect the overall portfolio. Effective risk management:

Prevents large drawdowns: It ensures that no single loss can have a devastating impact on your account.

Encourages disciplined trading: It aligns with a trader's predefined rules, removing emotional decisions.

Preserves capital: By managing risk, traders protect their capital, which allows them to participate in future opportunities.

Key Risk Management Principles

1. The 1-2% Rule

The 1-2% rule is a common risk management guideline stating that no more than 1-2% of your total account balance should be at risk in any single trade. This ensures that a single losing trade has a minimal effect on the overall account.

Example: If you have a $10,000 trading account, risking 1% per trade means you can only risk $100 on any one trade. If a trade goes against you, it only reduces your account by a small amount.

2. Risk-to-Reward Ratio

The risk-to-reward ratio compares the potential profit of a trade to the potential loss. Most traders aim for a minimum 1:2 or 1:3 risk-to-reward ratio, meaning they are willing to risk $1 for the opportunity to earn $2 or $3.

Example: Let's say you identify a trade with a $50 risk (difference between entry and stop-loss) and a $150 potential profit. This gives you a 1:3 risk-to-reward ratio, a favorable setup that ensures that a few profitable trades will offset multiple losses.

3. Setting Stop-Loss and Take-Profit Orders

A stop-loss is an order that automatically closes your position when it reaches a specified price, limiting potential losses. Similarly, a take-profit order automatically closes your trade when it hits a predefined profit target.

Example: You buy a stock at $100, with a stop-loss at $95 and a take-profit at $115. If the stock drops to $95, the stop-loss triggers, minimizing your loss. If it hits $115, you lock in profits without constantly monitoring the trade.

4. Position Sizing

Position sizing determines how many units of an asset to buy or sell in a trade. Position size is crucial for controlling risk because it directly affects the dollar amount you stand to lose if a trade goes wrong.

Formula: Position Size = (Account Balance * Risk per Trade) / (Entry Price - Stop-Loss Price)

Example: With a $10,000 account and a risk of 1%, you're willing to lose $100 on a trade. If your entry price is $50 and your stop-loss is $48, your position size would be 50 units of the asset.

Common Risk Management Strategies

1. Diversification

Diversification is the practice of spreading investments across multiple assets to reduce exposure to any single risk. In trading, diversification can mean trading different asset classes (e.g., stocks, forex, commodities) or different sectors.

Example: A trader may allocate funds to stocks, bonds, and forex rather than putting all funds into one asset class, balancing risk among different types of assets.

2. Hedging

Hedging involves opening a second position to offset potential losses in the primary position. It's a protective strategy often used in volatile markets.

Example: If a trader holds a portfolio of tech stocks and anticipates short-term volatility, they might open a short position in a tech sector ETF to counterbalance potential losses.

3. Trailing Stop-Loss

A trailing stop-loss is a dynamic stop-loss that adjusts as the price moves in your favor. It helps lock in profits while letting the trade run as long as it's moving positively.

Example: You set a trailing stop-loss at 5% for a stock bought at $100. If the stock price rises to $110, the stop-loss moves up to $104.50 (5% below the current price), protecting profits if the price starts to fall.

Real-World Examples of Risk Management

Example 1: Warren Buffett's Approach to Risk

Warren Buffett is famous for saying, "Rule No. 1: Never lose money. Rule No. 2: Never forget Rule No. 1." His approach is centered on careful analysis, long-term value investing, and avoiding unnecessary risks. Rather than chasing high returns, Buffett focuses on capital preservation and steady growth.

Example 2: George Soros' Reflexivity Theory

George Soros is known for taking large positions, but he also advocates for understanding market reflexivity, where asset prices influence market fundamentals. His risk management strategy often involves adjusting his positions based on evolving conditions, maintaining flexibility rather than rigid stop-losses.

Building a Personal Risk Management Plan

Define Your Risk Tolerance: Risk tolerance varies depending on financial goals, trading style, and capital. New traders may have lower risk tolerance, while experienced traders might be comfortable with higher risk.

Set Clear Stop-Loss and Take-Profit Levels: These levels help enforce discipline, preventing emotional decision-making in volatile markets.

Use a Trading Journal: A trading journal helps track trades, outcomes, and lessons learned. By recording trade details and reflections, traders can review and refine their strategies over time.

Adjust Position Sizes Based on Market Volatility: Volatile markets may require smaller position sizes to control risk, while calm markets can allow for slightly larger positions without increasing exposure.

Common Risk Management Mistakes

Not Using a Stop-Loss: Not having a stop-loss is one of the quickest ways to experience large losses. It's essential to set a stop-loss on every trade.

Overleveraging: Using excessive leverage can lead to significant losses. Staying within manageable leverage limits keeps risks controlled.

Ignoring Market Conditions: Different market conditions, like high volatility or low liquidity, can greatly impact risk. Adjusting strategies for changing market environments is crucial.

Conclusion

Risk management isn't just a defensive strategy—it's a path to consistent, sustainable profitability. By setting clear boundaries on losses, calculating risk-to-reward ratios, and adhering to disciplined practices, traders create a foundation for long-term success. This chapter emphasizes that managing risk is as essential as identifying profitable opportunities, and in many cases, it is the very factor that determines trading longevity.

As you progress through this book and explore advanced trading techniques, remember that risk management is the backbone of every successful trading system. It's not about avoiding risk altogether but learning how to handle it in a way that secures your position in the market, allowing you to grow your capital steadily over time. In the next chapter, we'll look at trade psychology and mindset, elements that are deeply intertwined with effective risk management.

OUR CONTACT LINKS

[**WWW.RETROTRADING.ONLINE**] OUR WEBSITE

RETRO_TRADING_ [INSTA]

[https://www.instagram.com/retro_trading_/profilecard/?igsh=N3hvaWNlbGo4bGd2]

IX

Building a Trading Plan

A well-defined trading plan is the blueprint for successful trading. It is a strategic, structured outline of how you approach trading, setting out clear rules, objectives, risk management parameters, and evaluation criteria. In this chapter, we'll walk through the elements that make up a strong trading plan, ensuring it's robust enough to guide decisions, flexible enough to adapt to changing market conditions, and effective in fostering consistent profitability.

Why is a Trading Plan Essential?

Creating a trading plan is essential because it serves as a roadmap, helping you navigate the emotional and financial ups and downs of the market. Trading without a plan is akin to setting sail without a destination or navigation tools. Here are some key reasons a trading plan is essential:

Discipline: A trading plan enforces discipline, reducing impulsive decisions that often lead to losses.

Consistency: By following a structured approach, you can assess performance over time and adjust strategies accordingly.

Risk Control: It sets predefined rules for risk, helping to prevent significant losses.

Emotional Management: A clear plan reduces the emotional impact of trading, providing a calming framework during stressful times.

Elements of a Strong Trading Plan

1. Defining Your Trading Goals

The first step in building a trading plan is setting clear, realistic goals. Think about both short-term and long-term objectives:

Short-term goals: Monthly or quarterly profit targets.

Long-term goals: Yearly targets or even multi-year objectives, such as creating a sustainable source of income.

2. Identifying Your Trading Style

Each trader's personality suits a different trading style. Identifying your trading style is crucial because it determines the types of trades you'll make, your level of market engagement, and your risk tolerance.

Day Trading: Involves buying and selling within the same day, suitable for traders who can dedicate hours to actively monitoring the market.

Swing Trading: Holding trades for several days to weeks, ideal for those who prefer medium-term opportunities.

Position Trading: Longer-term trades based on trends and fundamentals, typically held for months.

Scalping: Fast trades that capture small profits in minutes, suited for highly focused traders who thrive on quick decision-making.

3. Setting Risk Management Rules

Risk management is a non-negotiable part of any trading plan. Effective risk management keeps losses small while allowing profits to grow.

Risk Per Trade: Determine the maximum percentage of your capital you are willing to risk on a single trade (often between 1-2%).

Daily Loss Limit: Set a limit for daily losses. For instance, if you reach a 3% loss in a day, stop trading for the day.

Position Sizing: Calculate the ideal number of units to buy or sell based on your risk level and stop-loss distance.

4. Establishing Entry and Exit Criteria

Define specific entry and exit criteria that align with your trading strategy. This part of the plan specifies when to enter a trade and when to exit, aiming to maximize profit while limiting risk.

Entry Criteria: Identify conditions that must be met before entering a trade, such as price action setups, indicators, or chart patterns.

Exit Criteria: Define when to take profits or cut losses. This includes setting stop-loss levels, trailing stops, and profit targets based on risk-to-reward ratios.

5. Choosing Markets and Instruments

Decide which markets and instruments align with your skills, knowledge, and resources. Each market has unique characteristics, liquidity, volatility, and hours of operation.

Forex: Highly liquid and open 24 hours, but influenced by global economic data.

Stocks: Requires understanding company fundamentals and market cycles.

Commodities: Driven by global supply and demand, geopolitical events, and economic indicators.

Cryptocurrency: High volatility, ideal for speculative strategies but requiring high-risk tolerance.

Creating a Detailed Trading Strategy

Once the basic framework is set, focus on the technical and fundamental analysis components that guide your trade decisions. The strategy should include:

Technical Analysis: Define which indicators, tools, and chart patterns you'll use to identify trading opportunities (e.g., moving averages, RSI, candlestick patterns).

Fundamental Analysis: Outline the fundamental factors you consider, such as earnings reports for stocks, interest rates for forex, or supply and demand for commodities.

Backtesting: Test your strategy using historical data to validate its effectiveness before applying it in live markets.

Example of a Simple Strategy

Imagine you're a swing trader using a moving average crossover strategy. Your plan might look like this:

Entry Signal: Buy when the 50-day moving average crosses above the 200-day moving average, with the RSI showing a reading above 50.

Exit Signal: Sell when the 50-day moving average crosses back below the 200-day moving average or when the RSI drops below 50.

Risk Management: Place a stop-loss 2% below the entry price and a profit target 6% above.

Trading Journal and Performance Evaluation

A trading journal is crucial for tracking and analyzing trades over time. This record-keeping tool provides valuable insights and helps refine strategies.

Recording Trades: Document each trade's date, entry and exit points, position size, profit/loss, and any notes on strategy effectiveness.

Analyzing Performance: Regularly review your trading journal to identify patterns in both winning and losing trades.

Adjusting the Plan: Use insights from your journal to fine-tune your trading plan and strategies.

Psychological Aspects of a Trading Plan

Trading psychology plays a significant role in sticking to a plan, especially during volatile market conditions. Include tactics for managing emotions:

Managing Fear and Greed: Establish rules for when to step away from the market to avoid impulsive trades driven by emotions.

Developing Patience: Trust your plan rather than rushing into trades that don't meet your criteria.

Handling Losses: Accept that losses are part of trading, and avoid revenge trading to recoup losses.

Strategies for Different Market Conditions

Markets go through different phases, including uptrends, downtrends, and sideways movements. Tailor your plan to adapt to these conditions:

Trending Markets: In trending conditions, use strategies like moving average crossovers or trendline bounces.

Range-Bound Markets: Employ range trading strategies, buying at support and selling at resistance.

High Volatility: In high volatility, focus on quick trades with tight stops or consider using options strategies to hedge against sudden movements.

Reviewing and Evolving the Trading Plan

A strong trading plan isn't static. Regular reviews ensure that it adapts to changes in the market and in your trading skills:

Weekly and Monthly Reviews: Evaluate trades over different timeframes to assess strategy effectiveness.

Adjusting to Market Changes: For example, if volatility increases, adjust position sizes or use wider stop-losses.

Incorporating New Knowledge: As you learn new strategies or techniques, integrate them into your plan with thorough testing.

Example of a Trading Plan Outline

Trading Goals: Achieve a 3% monthly return with a 1% maximum risk per trade.

Trading Style: Swing trading, holding positions for several days.

Risk Management:

Max risk per trade: 1% of capital

Position size based on stop-loss

Stop trading if daily loss exceeds 2%

Market and Instruments: Focus on forex major pairs (e.g., EUR/USD, GBP/USD).

Entry Criteria: Bullish reversal candlestick patterns with RSI above 50.

Exit Criteria: Trailing stop with a 3:1 risk-to-reward ratio.

Trading Psychology: Take a break after three consecutive losses, review trading journal weekly.

Conclusion

Building a strong trading plan is foundational to achieving consistency and success in trading. It provides a structured approach to decision-making, encompassing goals, risk management, market selection, strategies, and psychological preparation. Remember, a trading plan is only as good as the trader's commitment to follow it. By setting clear guidelines and continuously refining your approach, you build the resilience and skill necessary to navigate markets confidently.

In the next chapter, we'll explore the role of psychology in trading—understanding how emotions influence decisions and developing the mindset essential for long-term success in trading.

ꟸ

OUR CONTACT LINKS

[**WWW.RETROTRADING.ONLINE**] OUR WEBSITE

RETRO_TRADING_ [INSTA]

[https://www.instagram.com/retro_trading_/profilecard/?igsh=N3hvaWNlbGo4bGd2]

X

Common Mistakes and How to Avoid Them

Trading, while potentially lucrative, is fraught with common pitfalls. Mistakes in trading don't just lead to financial loss; they can damage a trader's confidence and lead to a negative mindset. Knowing the common mistakes traders make—and more importantly, understanding how to avoid them—is a key part of building a successful trading career. In this chapter, we'll explore some of the most frequently encountered mistakes, strategies to avoid them, and real-world examples to highlight the importance of consistent, disciplined trading.

Trading Without a Plan

One of the most frequent errors is entering the market without a solid trading plan. Trading without a plan leads to impulsive decisions, inconsistent results, and, ultimately, frustration.

Solution

Develop a Clear Trading Plan: Start by outlining a clear plan that includes goals, risk tolerance, entry/exit criteria, and rules for position sizing. This plan acts as a roadmap and helps maintain discipline during volatile periods.

Stick to the Plan: Avoid deviating from your plan based on emotions or market news. Evaluate and adjust your plan over time, but stick to it rigorously once you're in a trade.

Example

Imagine a trader who jumps into trades whenever they hear about a stock or currency "about to explode." They may experience a few lucky trades, but without a structured plan, their gains are likely unsustainable. Traders who approach the market with a solid, repeatable plan consistently outperform impulsive traders.

2. Ignoring Risk Management

Risk management is one of the pillars of successful trading. Ignoring risk management, such as not setting stop-losses or trading with excessive leverage, is a common pitfall that leads to significant losses.

Solution

Use Stop-Loss Orders: A stop-loss is an essential risk management tool that limits potential losses. Set your stop-loss based on your risk tolerance, and never move it in a direction that increases risk.

Position Sizing: Avoid risking more than 1-2% of your trading capital on a single trade. Calculate your position size based on the distance to your stop-loss level.

Avoid Overleveraging: Leverage magnifies both gains and losses. Start with lower leverage and increase it only once you've demonstrated consistent profitability with solid risk control.

Example

Consider a trader who leverages their account to take larger positions. One unexpected market move wipes out their account balance. Traders who practice responsible leverage and position sizing weather these moves without severe financial impact.

Overtrading

Overtrading is a common mistake, especially for beginners eager to make quick profits. It involves taking too many trades or trading excessively large positions, often without sound analysis.

Solution

Set Limits on Daily/Weekly Trades: Decide on a maximum number of trades per day or week. This limit will prevent unnecessary trades and improve the quality of your trading setups.

Take Only High-Probability Setups: Wait for trades that meet all your criteria. Don't trade out of boredom or FOMO (Fear of Missing Out).

Focus on Quality Over Quantity: Trading less can sometimes yield more, as it allows you to focus on high-quality setups and analyze the market more deeply.

Example

A trader who enters multiple trades daily based on minor signals ends up eroding their account through fees and inconsistent results. By trading only high-probability setups, they increase their chances of profitable trades.

4. Letting Emotions Dictate Decisions

Trading involves substantial emotional highs and lows. Letting emotions dictate decisions can lead to revenge trading, hesitation, or early exits, which are detrimental to consistency.

Solution

Follow the Plan and Avoid Emotional Trades: Trust the research and analysis that went into creating your trading plan.

Use Mindfulness Techniques: Techniques like deep breathing, meditation, and pausing before decisions can help manage emotions.

Take Breaks: If you experience several losses, step back to clear your mind. Avoid revenge trading, which is often emotionally driven.

Example

A trader who experiences a losing streak decides to "win it all back" with a larger trade, only to face further losses. Practicing mindfulness and emotional discipline helps traders avoid this cycle.

5. Lack of Patience

Impatience can lead to entering trades too early, exiting too soon, or not waiting for a setup to fully develop. Patience is a core component of consistent trading.

Solution

Set Entry Triggers: Define specific conditions that must be met before entering a trade. This discipline helps you avoid premature entries.

Use Alerts: Set price alerts instead of monitoring charts constantly. Alerts can help you wait for the right moment without overanalyzing or acting impulsively.

Follow the Market Rhythm: Observe how long setups usually take to form and adjust your mindset to match this timeframe.

Example

A trader who consistently exits trades at the first sign of resistance misses out on long-term profit. By practicing patience, they allow trades to reach their true potential.

6. Failing to Keep a Trading Journal

Many traders skip maintaining a journal of their trades, losing out on valuable insights into their own trading behavior and strategy effectiveness.

Solution

Document Every Trade: Record entry and exit points, the rationale behind the trade, position size, outcome, and any emotional reactions. Include screenshots or notes for context.

Review Regularly: Look back over your journal monthly or quarterly to identify patterns, such as consistently profitable setups or common mistakes.

Use the Journal to Adjust Your Strategy: Over time, your journal will reveal what's working and what isn't, allowing you to refine your plan.

Example

A trader who documents each trade notices that they consistently make profitable entries but tend to exit prematurely. By reviewing this pattern, they adjust their strategy to hold positions longer, improving their overall performance.

7. Ignoring Market Conditions

Market conditions can vary significantly, and using the same strategy in all conditions often results in losses. A common mistake is failing to adapt to changing markets.

Solution

Recognize Market Phases: Understand whether the market is trending, ranging, or experiencing high volatility, and adjust your strategy accordingly.

Use Indicators to Gauge Market Conditions: Moving averages, volume, and volatility indicators help identify market conditions.

Develop Different Strategies for Different Conditions: For example, use trend-following strategies during strong trends and range-trading strategies when markets are choppy.

Example

A trend trader who enters the market during a ranging period experiences multiple losses. By identifying and respecting market phases, they avoid forcing trend strategies in non-trending conditions.

8. Chasing Trades or "FOMO"

Fear of missing out (FOMO) is a major emotional driver that pushes traders into suboptimal trades. Chasing after trades usually results in entries that are too late or at poor price levels.

Solution

Wait for Pullbacks: Instead of entering trades at peak levels, wait for a retracement or a pullback to a support/resistance level.

Develop a Balanced Perspective: Remind yourself that there will always be another opportunity in the market.

Set Clear Entry Criteria: Follow your criteria without allowing the fear of missing out to alter your decisions.

Example

A trader sees a rapid price spike and enters at the top, only to watch the price retrace immediately. By waiting for a pullback, they could enter at a more favorable price.

9. Mismanaging Leverage

Many traders use leverage excessively, increasing both their potential gains and their risk exposure. This is especially problematic for beginners who may not fully understand the impact of leverage on their trades.

Solution

Understand Leverage Ratios: Learn about leverage ratios and choose a conservative one that aligns with your risk tolerance.

Limit Leverage for High-Volatility Markets: For volatile markets, reduce leverage to minimize risk.

Start Small: Begin with low leverage, and only increase it as you gain more experience and consistent profitability.

Example

A novice trader using high leverage faces a significant loss on a small market move. Experienced traders avoid this pitfall by using leverage prudently, aligning with market conditions.

Conclusion

Avoiding common trading mistakes requires awareness, discipline, and ongoing self-reflection. By creating a robust trading plan, adhering to risk management principles, maintaining emotional control, and continuously learning from each trade, you set yourself on a path toward consistent profitability. Embrace each mistake as a learning opportunity, and remember that true growth in trading comes from refining your strategy based on real-world experience.

In the next chapter, we will explore advanced technical analysis tools and indicators that can further refine your approach to trading, empowering you with the knowledge to interpret market signals with greater accuracy.

ꟸ

OUR CONTACT LINKS

[**WWW.RETROTRADING.ONLINE**] OUR WEBSITE

RETRO_TRADING_ [INSTA]

[https://www.instagram.com/retro_trading_/profilecard/?igsh=N3hvaWNlbGo4bGd2]

XI

Conclusion and Next Steps

As you complete this guide on trading fundamentals and advanced techniques, you've gained a comprehensive understanding of the essential concepts that underpin successful trading. From learning how to read charts and patterns to developing solid entry and exit strategies, building a trading plan, and practicing disciplined risk management, you're now equipped with the tools needed to navigate the markets effectively.

Key Takeaways

Foundations are Crucial: Mastery in trading begins with a strong understanding of the basics. Knowing how to interpret candlestick patterns, recognizing trends, and analyzing chart patterns forms the backbone of a sound trading approach.

Risk Management as a Priority: Effective risk management protects your trading capital, ensuring you can endure losses without compromising your ability to trade. Adopting stop-loss orders, position sizing, and managing leverage are essential practices that should be incorporated into every trade.

The Importance of a Trading Plan: Your trading plan is your blueprint for success. It keeps you disciplined and aligned with your financial goals, risk tolerance, and personal trading style. Sticking to your plan, even during periods of market volatility, helps maintain a consistent and professional approach.

Continuous Learning and Adaptation: Markets are dynamic, and strategies that work today may not be as effective tomorrow. Keep an open mind and commit to continuous learning, reviewing past trades, refining strategies, and adapting to changing market conditions.

Mindset and Discipline: Trading requires emotional resilience and patience. Avoiding common mistakes like overtrading, chasing trades, and letting emotions dictate decisions is crucial for long-term success. Cultivate a mindset of discipline, reflection, and objectivity.

Next Steps

As you transition from learning to practical application, consider these next steps to reinforce your trading journey:

Practice in a Demo Account: Before trading with real money, test your strategies in a demo account. This provides a risk-free environment to apply what you've learned, refine your methods, and gain confidence without financial pressure.

Start Small and Scale Gradually: When you're ready to trade live, start with smaller trades and gradually scale as you build consistency. Avoid the temptation to increase position sizes too quickly.

Maintain a Trading Journal: Document each trade, including entry/exit points, strategy, and emotions. Over time, your journal becomes a valuable resource for identifying strengths, areas for improvement, and patterns in your trading behavior.

Engage in Continued Education: Trading is a lifelong journey, and the most successful traders never stop learning. Engage in continued education through books, online courses, webinars, and forums. Following market news and economic events also sharpens your understanding of broader market influences.

Stay Connected with the Trading Community: Interacting with other traders can provide new insights, expose you to different perspectives, and keep you motivated. Consider joining online trading communities, attending seminars, or participating in webinars to stay connected.

Review and Revise Your Trading Plan Regularly: Markets evolve, and so should your trading plan. Schedule periodic reviews of your plan, incorporating insights from your trading journal and any new strategies you've developed.

Final Thoughts

Trading is both a science and an art, requiring a blend of technical skill and mental discipline. It offers endless learning opportunities, and with dedication, patience, and a clear focus on risk management, you can carve out your unique path to trading success. Mistakes and setbacks are part of the journey; treat them as learning experiences that make you a better trader over time.

Your trading journey will be filled with challenges and rewards. Embrace both with a growth mindset, and remember that success in trading comes through patience, practice, and perseverance. As you embark on this journey, stay curious, disciplined, and resilient.

In the end, your success as a trader depends on consistency, self-discipline, and a commitment to continuous improvement. Happy trading, and may your journey in the markets be both profitable and fulfilling!

ꕥ

OUR CONTACT LINKS

[**WWW.RETROTRADING.ONLINE**] OUR WEBSITE

RETRO_TRADING_ [INSTA]

[https://www.instagram.com/retro_trading_/profilecard/?igsh=N3hvaWNlbGo4bGd2]

XII
EXAM

Section 1: Basics of Trading and Price Action (Chapters 1–2)

Multiple Choice

What does "price action" primarily refer to in trading?

A) Price levels only

B) The movement of prices over time

C) News events affecting the market

D) Market volume

Which of the following best describes a "candlestick" in trading?

A) An indicator showing only the open price of an asset

B) A chart pattern representing the price movement within a specific time frame

C) A tool used to draw support lines

D) A volume-based indicator

Short Answer

Define "price action" and explain why it is crucial for traders to understand.

Why is it essential to learn the basics of price action before using complex indicators?

Section 2: Reading Candlesticks and Charts (Chapter 3)

Multiple Choice

A green candlestick typically indicates:

A) The price closed lower than it opened

B) The price closed higher than it opened

C) No change in price

D) None of the above

Which candlestick pattern is often associated with a potential reversal in a downtrend?

A) Doji

B) Hammer

C) Engulfing pattern

D) Shooting star

Scenario-Based

You observe a bullish engulfing pattern on a daily chart. Explain what this suggests about the market sentiment and the potential action you might take.

Describe the difference between a "Doji" and a "Hammer" candlestick, and explain the trading implications of each.

Section 3: Support and Resistance (Chapter 4)

Multiple Choice

Support is typically viewed as:

A) A price level where the asset has difficulty going above

B) A price level where the asset tends to reverse upward

C) A chart pattern signaling a downtrend

D) A short-term price fluctuation

If a price level breaks through a resistance line, this is known as a:

A) Reversal

B) Breakout

C) Pullback

D) Support test

Short Answer

How do you identify a support level on a chart, and why is it important?

Explain the concept of "resistance" and describe a scenario where it might turn into support.

Section 4: Trends and Trendlines (Chapter 5)

Multiple Choice

A series of higher highs and higher lows indicates:

A) A sideways market

B) A downtrend

C) An uptrend

D) No trend

When drawing an uptrend line, you connect:

A) The peaks of the price movements

B) The lows of the price movements

C) Both the peaks and lows

D) Only the closing prices

Scenario-Based

You notice that an asset is moving in a clear downtrend. How might you apply trendlines to help inform your trading decisions?

Explain the difference between a "pullback" in a trend and a "trend reversal."

Section 5: Chart Patterns (Chapter 6)

Multiple Choice

A "head and shoulders" pattern typically signals:

A) A continuation

B) A reversal

C) No significant change

D) A breakout

A "triangle" pattern often indicates:

A) A consolidation phase

B) An immediate reversal

C) No particular trend

D) High volatility

Short Answer

Describe the difference between a "double top" and a "double bottom" pattern.

Why is it essential to confirm chart patterns with additional analysis?

Section 6: Entry and Exit Strategies (Chapter 7)

Multiple Choice

What is a common mistake traders make with entry points?

A) Entering without any technical analysis

B) Relying too much on stop-loss orders

C) Entering only after extensive backtesting

D) All of the above

When choosing an exit strategy, you should consider:

A) Only your entry point

B) Your desired risk-to-reward ratio

C) Market news only

D) Avoiding stop-losses

Scenario-Based

You're considering entering a trade in an uptrend but notice resistance nearby. How might this impact your entry strategy?

Explain why it's vital to have an exit strategy before entering a trade.

Section 7: Risk Management (Chapter 8)

Multiple Choice

Risk-to-reward ratio helps traders by:

A) Allowing them to set realistic profit goals

B) Ensuring they never lose on a trade

C) Letting them ignore support levels

D) Minimizing drawdowns completely

Which of the following is NOT a component of risk management?

A) Position sizing

B) Diversification

C) Ignoring market news

D) Setting stop-loss levels

Short Answer

Describe what "position sizing" is and why it's important in risk management.

Why is a stop-loss essential for every trade?

Section 8: Building a Strong Trading Plan (Chapter 9)

Multiple Choice

A good trading plan includes:

A) Only a clear entry strategy

B) Both entry and exit strategies, along with risk management

C) Emotional trading tactics

D) Following other traders blindly

Reviewing and updating your trading plan is essential because:

A) Market conditions change

B) It's required by law

C) It ensures every trade is profitable

D) None of the above

Scenario-Based

If a trade doesn't align with your trading plan, what should you do?

Why is it important to document your trades and review them?

Section 9: Common Mistakes and How to Avoid Them (Chapter 10)

Multiple Choice

A common mistake traders make is:

A) Overtrading

B) Setting stop-losses

C) Sticking to their trading plan

D) Using a risk-to-reward ratio

Failing to practice backtesting can lead to:

A) Greater understanding of your strategy

B) Fewer mistakes

C) A lack of confidence in your strategy

D) A stronger trading plan

Short Answer

Explain why emotional trading can be dangerous.

List three strategies for avoiding impulsive trading decisions.

Reflection and Next Steps

Complete this exam as honestly as possible, and use it as a tool for identifying areas where you may need further study or practice. Trading is a lifelong learning process, and this assessment will help reinforce your strengths and clarify areas for continued development. Remember, trading success comes with patience, discipline, and a dedication to continuous improvement. Good luck!

ANSWERS

Section 1: Basics of Trading and Price Action (Chapters 1–2)

Multiple Choice

B) The movement of prices over time

B) A chart pattern representing the price movement within a specific time frame

Short Answer

Price action refers to the analysis of historical price movements to make trading decisions, helping traders read the "story" of market behavior without relying on lagging indicators.

Understanding price action is foundational because it provides a pure view of market sentiment and trends, allowing traders to make informed decisions without overcomplicating strategies with technical indicators.

Section 2: Reading Candlesticks and Charts (Chapter 3)

Multiple Choice

B) The price closed higher than it opened

B) Hammer

Scenario-Based

A bullish engulfing pattern suggests a potential upward reversal, showing that buyers are gaining control. Traders might consider this as an entry signal in a bullish direction.

A Doji indicates indecision, while a Hammer often suggests a reversal. Dojis usually signal a pause, and hammers indicate that buyers have rejected lower prices, which can imply an upcoming reversal.

Section 3: Support and Resistance (Chapter 4)

Multiple Choice

B) A price level where the asset tends to reverse upward

B) Breakout

Short Answer

To identify support, look for areas on the chart where prices have bounced upward multiple times. Support levels are important as they help traders set entry and stop-loss points.

Resistance represents a price ceiling where an asset struggles to go higher. After a breakout above resistance, it can turn into support, signifying a potential entry level.

Section 4: Trends and Trendlines (Chapter 5)

Multiple Choice

C) An uptrend

B) The lows of the price movements

Scenario-Based

In a downtrend, trendlines can help in setting resistance levels for short positions. Following a break above the trendline might indicate a trend reversal.

A pullback is a temporary retracement, while a trend reversal signals a potential change in direction. Pullbacks are part of a trend; reversals imply a trend change.

Section 5: Chart Patterns (Chapter 6)

Multiple Choice

B) A reversal

A) A consolidation phase

Short Answer

A double top is a bearish reversal pattern; a double bottom is bullish, signaling potential upward movement after reaching a second low.

Chart patterns should be confirmed with other forms of analysis, such as volume, to validate the pattern and reduce the risk of false signals.

Section 6: Entry and Exit Strategies (Chapter 7)

Multiple Choice

A) Entering without any technical analysis

B) Your desired risk-to-reward ratio

Scenario-Based

With resistance nearby, you might wait for a breakout or consider a tighter stop-loss to manage risk.

An exit strategy ensures a trader has a plan to secure profits or cut losses. This prevents emotional decision-making during trades.

Section 7: Risk Management (Chapter 8)

Multiple Choice

A) Allowing them to set realistic profit goals

C) Ignoring market news

Short Answer

Position sizing is determining the amount to invest in each trade. It's crucial for managing risk and ensuring losses stay within a tolerable range.

A stop-loss minimizes loss by closing a trade if it moves against you. It's a key part of risk management.

Section 8: Building a Strong Trading Plan (Chapter 9)

Multiple Choice

B) Both entry and exit strategies, along with risk management

A) Market conditions change

Scenario-Based

If a trade doesn't match your plan, you should avoid it, staying disciplined to prevent impulsive actions.

Documenting trades helps track performance, refine strategies, and learn from past mistakes.

Section 9: Common Mistakes and How to Avoid Them (Chapter 10)

Multiple Choice

A) Overtrading

C) A lack of confidence in your strategy

Short Answer

Emotional trading can lead to irrational decisions, like chasing losses or ignoring strategies, increasing risk.

Avoid impulsive trading by setting rules, practicing patience, and reviewing your plan before every trade.

This answer key should help you review and better understand the critical concepts of trading covered in each chapter. Taking the time to analyze and apply these answers to real trading scenarios will deepen your knowledge and improve your confidence as a trader.

OUR CONTACT LINKS

[**WWW.RETROTRADING.ONLINE**] OUR WEBSITE

RETRO_TRADING_ [INSTA]

[https://www.instagram.com/retro_trading_/profilecard/?igsh=N3hvaWNlbGo4bGd2]

Glossary

To aid readers in fully understanding the terms discussed in this book, here's a glossary of key trading concepts:

Price Action: The movement of an asset's price over time, without the use of technical indicators, to make trading decisions.

Candlestick Patterns: Visual representations of price movement within a specific period, showing open, high, low, and close prices.

Support and Resistance: Levels where prices repeatedly stop falling (support) or stop rising (resistance).

Risk Management: Strategies to protect trading capital by managing losses and gains, including position sizing and stop-losses.

Trend: The overall direction of price movement, categorized as uptrend, downtrend, or sideways.

Breakout: When the price moves beyond a defined support or resistance level, often leading to significant price movement.

Further Reading

For those looking to deepen their knowledge, here are some resources that complement the topics discussed in this book:

"Technical Analysis of the Financial Markets" by John Murphy – A comprehensive guide to technical analysis.

"Japanese Candlestick Charting Techniques" by Steve Nison – A deep dive into candlestick charting.

"Trade Your Way to Financial Freedom" by Van K. Tharp – Insightful strategies on creating personalized trading systems.

Online Trading Platforms – Many trading platforms offer tutorials and simulated trading environments that allow for practice in real market conditions.

Acknowledgments

I want to express my profound gratitude to everyone who has contributed to this journey. To my family, for their unwavering support. To my mentors, whose guidance has been invaluable. And to my students, who continue to inspire me to share knowledge and improve. This book is dedicated to all of you, as you have made this journey possible.

Index

About the Author

With a career spanning over six years in the world of trading, Haffizulla Khan has devoted countless hours to mastering the art of price action and training thousands of students in various global markets. From humble beginnings in Bangalore, I built a reputation as a dedicated trader and educator who emphasizes the importance of disciplined trading and practical knowledge. This book reflects khan's deep commitment to demystifying trading for aspiring traders worldwide.

For further insights, trading resources, and updates, you can connect with RETRO_TRADING_ on social media or visit their website at [https://www.instagram.com/ retro_trading_/profilecard/?igsh=N3hvaWNlbGo4bGd2].

Afterword

Trading is more than just financial transactions; it's a journey of self-discovery, discipline, and resilience. I hope that through "Price Action Insights," you've gained a toolkit for understanding the markets and developed the confidence to trade with clarity and purpose. Remember, success in trading is not a destination but a continuous journey of learning and improvement. Let this be the beginning of a fulfilling path in the markets.

Thank you for reading, and I wish you the best on your trading journey.

OUR CONTACT LINKS

[**WWW.RETROTRADING.ONLINE**] OUR WEBSITE

RETRO_TRADING_ [INSTA]

[https://www.instagram.com/ retro_trading_/profilecard/?igsh=N3hvaWNlbGo4bGd2]